Thanks Jim !

W9-AOP-900

IF THAT CAR COULD TALK

How to Locate and Maintain a Good Used Car

JOE BOULAY

outskirtspress

DENVER, COLORADO

Table of Contents

Foreword

I dedicate this book to my Mom and Dad, Carol F. Boulay and Maurice V. Boulay. If it were not for them I would not be here today.

During the many years that I have been in the automotive repair field, I have seen many people not take the time required to find a safe, dependable automobile. I have also seen many cases where individuals have made the same mistake when shopping for good-quality controlled automotive service and repair. It has disturbed me greatly over the years to continually see good honest people get taken for a ride when purchasing a new or used car, or when getting it repaired and maintained. Many vehicles on the road today are labeled unreliable, or money pits, etc. I believe these vehicles have been given this label because they have been poorly maintained. My hope is that this book will help you learn how to spot a well-maintained used vehicle, purchase it, and keep it well-maintained as long as you own it. I have written this book for you—I hope you enjoy it!

Thank you.
Joe P. Boulay

Acknowledgements

I would like to first thank my wife, Melinda, my best friend and soul mate for all her support and patience throughout the process of writing this book, even with our busy, sometimes hectic schedules! Without her support this book would not be possible. All of my love to my daughter Jillian, you have changed my life.

I would like to thank many people in my life that have influenced me positively as a person and a mechanic over the years, some I have worked for, some I have worked with, and some are just good friends.

I would like to thank Scott Trendell for giving me the positive input and direction needed to guide me through the process of writing this book. You have inspired and pointed me towards a bright and optimistic future.

I would like to extend great appreciation to Karen Trendell, you are awesome!

I would like to mention all of the people that have influenced me through my life in a positive way. I would like to show my gratitude and thank all of you by listing your names below.

Alan Anderson, Bill Harris, Brian Gill, Bruce Lyon, Bryon (Augie) Austin, Bob Stowell, Bud Maynard, Christine Larson, Calvin Reini, David Taylor, Dave Gauffin, Ed (Buggy) Fleming, Eric Martin, Gary Allard, Gary Sawyer S.R, George Abby, Greg Getty, Jim Lavalley, Jackie Stromgren, Jeff Gauouette, Jeanie Usereau, Jim Rowse, James Ryan,

John Boccalini, Janet Boccalini, John Aremburg, Tim Hartwell, Tim Deel, Leon Watkins, Marc Hull, Malcolm Hull, Mike Hull, Mike Bresnahan, Mike Chase, Paul Maligutti, Randy Hastings, Randy Burroughs, Ray Forbes, Ron Savard, Donna Savard, Roy Carroll, Olive Carroll, Scott Crowl, Skip Marsh, Ted Athanasoupolous, Tim Austin, Tom Maynard, William Fenton, Winfred Savard. These people changed me for the better, I am grateful to know all of you.

Introduction

I n 1985 I started my career as an automotive technician. A lot has changed since then as far as technology and automotive engineering go. Unfortunately, not much has changed when someone is looking to purchase a new or used vehicle, or when bringing their vehicle in for repairs or routine maintenance. What has not changed, you may ask? The intimidation that many people feel when they want to purchase a new or used vehicle, or when, during routine maintenance, they have a service sold to them that they are told their car needs to have done now, when actually it does not need to be done right away.

I would say at least dozen or more times a year, customers will bring used cars for me to check over before they purchase from a dealership or used car lot, to see what *really needs to be done.* Sadly enough, some customers will bring in a car to have it checked over, *after they have purchased it,* and I don't usually have too much "good" news for them. This is just one of many reasons why I am writing this book for you.

For you, the customer, it is about THE EXPERIENCE you receive when you privilege a repair shop or dealership with your business when purchasing or servicing your vehicle. Remember, it's not just about fixing your car correctly the first time; it is about your OVERALL EXPERIENCE!

Well, suppose your car could talk, would you listen? In today's world, you may own a car that *does* talk to you. A lot of auto manufacturers have factory-installed voice command recognition systems. The system can be trained to recognize your voice, so you can command the radio on or off, or volume up and down. You can command your heating and air conditioning systems on and off, and so much more! Today's technology is really amazing! But still, the car is unable to tell you how it was treated by the person who owned it before. Maybe someday—who knows, right? But until your car can talk, let this book assist you in your search to find a good used car, and to find good maintenance and repair services to keep it safe and reliable.

CHAPTER 1
Your Very First Car

A s you read through this book it is important for you to understand that I am an automotive technician, not a car salesman.
I maintain and repair vehicles for a living, but I never lose sight of
how important my job is to keep cars safe and dependable. This
holds especially true for me when I see a baby seat secured in the
car I am about to work on. There are millions of vehicles on the road
today, and I am only one mechanic in the army of mechanics around

the world who keep them on the road safely. Thank your mechanic, especially if he or she is doing quality repairs or maintenance for you—they deserve it, and you will make their day!

From a mechanic's point of view I personally recommend you take notice of the makes and models of cars or trucks that are frequently hitching rides behind tow trucks. However, it would not be fair for me to point a finger entirely at any one automotive manufacturer for poor reliability. Owner abuse and lack of maintenance play major roles in automotive breakdowns in today's vehicles, but good engineering does help considerably. Remember this simple formula: Quality engineering + preventive maintenance = dependability. You must be aware that some vehicles will cost more to maintain properly. It is very important that you know up front what it is going to cost to own and maintain the car you are considering buying.

Quite often I will be approached by a friend, family member, or customer with this question: "Hey Joe, what do you think of this car or that truck?" I usually respond by saying, "Do you want me to take a look at it for you?" Most of the time, people want me to give them a positive answer right then and there because they have already put a down payment on the vehicle. In some cases they have already purchased the vehicle and neglected to have it checked out beforehand. Most of the time when an individual takes a chance and purchases a used car without having it checked over, they are confronted with some unpleasant surprises. At that point in time I can only be empathetic, not sympathetic, as they based their decision to buy a used car on impulse, with little or no thought put into the process. When you come right down to it, they have just purchased someone else's problems.

Unfortunately, this book will be of no help for the individuals who neglected to listen to me in the past, or for the ones who did not have their mechanic look their car over before they purchased it. My hope is to reach out and help individuals in the future before they make a poor decision when choosing a used car.

I am writing this book for many types of people, including the young person still in high school who is in the process of obtaining his or her driver's license and first vehicle. This chapter will also be beneficial for individuals who have owned many vehicles in their lifetime. If you have owned many cars in your life, let's try to imagine that this is your first car.

Everybody remembers the firsts in their life—your first girlfriend, boyfriend, or your first kiss. We all want good memories, not bad. We all go through learning curves in life, and I know the knowledge and wisdom that I have gained over the years will help you in a positive way when choosing a vehicle to purchase. As far as the relationship thing goes, you are on your own! My ultimate goal for you in this book is to have you benefit from my 25-plus years of experience in the automotive repair industry. I have pretty much seen it all, and I feel I need to share it with you.

You can learn so much from other people's good and bad experiences, when buying a new or used automobile. Many individuals will get taken advantage of when buying a new or used car. They say it will not happen again! Guess what? They go right back out and do the same thing over again! They do not take the time to find the right car for themselves. They may need to get another car as soon as possible, so they pay the price for not taking the time to do their homework searching for a good used car. Some individuals purchase a vehicle based on image. They want to be noticed, so they buy a car they are unable to afford. Inside, they may be secretly hoping that somebody or anybody will notice them as a rich, successful individual. No one really notices, so don't strap yourself financially trying to afford a vehicle you *really are unable to afford*. If you are looking for your first car and are worried about image, about looking cool, you may regret it later when you get your first repair bill—and don't forget the monthly payment on top of it. This does not exactly give you the warm fuzzies when reality sets in. We all want nice things, but don't break the bank trying to prove something to people around you. Do yourself a favor: Find a car that suits your needs.

Something irrational will happen to you when you see a car with a nice new paint job and shiny alloy wheels. You'll say to yourself, "I just have to own that car!" Remember this: You can put lipstick on a pig, but it is still a pig! You have to look beneath the surface and see the vehicle's true mechanical condition, in order to find a safe, reliable used vehicle. Do not let your emotions rule your decisions when looking for a good used car! Remember, your decision to purchase a vehicle may be based on 95% emotion and only 5% thought. If you do your homework, it has never been easier to find and purchase a new or used vehicle. We are now in the information age and it is everywhere, yet we still neglect to access it to our full advantage.

I am not saying you have to sacrifice getting a sporty car over a practical car, but it is all in how you approach it. Again, you have to look past the surface and into the mechanical aspects of the car to get the full value of what you want in a car. If you are not so moved by how a car looks and you just want a reliable car to get you from point A to point B, and you don't care what people think, that is even easier. In New England we call a car like that "a beater with a heater"! You must understand that a car like that may get you through only the cold winter months until you can get your nice car you put in for winter storage back on the road in the spring. Individuals who do this usually have an older classic car they drive in the summer months, driving another car of lesser value in the winter. This type of car can be a whole separate set of headaches in itself. You may have to cross your fingers and hope that the car will get you through the cold winter months without failure. I suggest that you focus on having one car to start with—one safe reliable car that won't let you down, especially if it is your very first car.

If all the used cars you looked at buying or bought could tell you how the previous owner treated them, you probably would not think of buying them. You see, a used car's condition is basically an extension of the person who previously owned it. Would you buy a car if you knew its previous owner drove straight into potholes in the road all the time? Or how about someone who changed their oil whenever they got around to it, if at all? Or how about the only way the car saw a mechanic is when something broke? If you could get this information, it would be easy to make your decision about what to buy or not to buy. We will talk more about previous owners in the chapter to follow.

One of my most important goals for you in this book is to have your very first car—or your tenth car—be a dependable, safe car. I want you to find a car that will get you safely back and forth without any major troubles. I want you to find a car that will not strap you with repair bill after repair bill, bleeding your wallet dry. It may sound a little extreme for me to say, but sometimes having dependable mobility can be the difference between success and failure in life. It has to be a positive experience for you to achieve your goals. You should not be traveling to college or your first job or your 100th job wondering if your car is going to break down. Then, how much it is going to cost you when it does break down? Most importantly, you should not have to worry about your car breaking down, resulting in an emergency situation.

So you have to ask yourself: "What do I want from a car?" If you have farm animals and you have to pick up grain or hay, you probably do not want a four-door Toyota Corolla, do you? That is a no-brainer; you would obviously need a truck for that. If you are going to college and you are going to be traveling long distances, you want something dependable and good on gas. In that case, you may be looking at buying a hybrid automobile, but you will pay a lot more for a hybrid car than you will for a straight gasoline-powered car. It is entirely up to you. You have to do your homework to see how long it is going to take to pay for itself from the money you save by purchasing less fuel. You may also get a tax credit from owning a hybrid automobile, so that could offset the extra expense of buying a hybrid, as well. Hopefully the government will continue to back that offer for some time.

You also need to remember that the batteries in a hybrid will need to be replaced; the estimated life is about ten years, so you will want to look into what it will cost you to replace the batteries. You also need to check on what it may cost you to properly dispose of the old batteries. How much will the batteries cost in ten years to replace? I have a customer at this point in time who needs to replace the batteries in his hybrid car. It will cost him over $2200 for the batteries alone. The other thing you must consider is that in ten years your hybrid vehicle may not be worth what it will cost you to invest in new batteries. You want to find this information out before you actually purchase a hybrid automobile.

I believe that hybrid vehicles are only a temporary Band-Aid for helping our environment, as far as pollution and fuel consumption are concerned. Don't get me wrong; hybrid vehicles do run cleaner than a vehicle that runs primarily on straight gasoline, but I believe that the vehicles of the future will be powered solely by hydrogen, or by solar power. The only thing that comes out of the tailpipe of a hydrogen-powered vehicle is H_2O. This could end our dependency on foreign oil and fossil fuels forever. The cost of mass producing hydrogen-powered vehicles needs to be reduced before this can become a reality. I think that hybrid vehicles are a good idea, but they are not the answer. If you are planning on putting on a lot of highway miles and want to keep your purchase price low, a small 4-cylinder car that uses less gasoline may be what you are looking for.

If you currently own a car, what do you like about the car? What do you not like about the car? You should give this some serious thought, especially if you plan on keeping the car for many years to come. Write down what you would like in your first car or your next car. If you have never owned a vehicle, ask someone who does. Ask them what they like or dislike about the current vehicle they own.

I would like to make one thing perfectly clear before you continue to read this book. If you are an "If it isn't broke don't fix it" type of person, then you should put this book down and go buy the first car that rolls in front of you. Cross your fingers and hope you have found a good car. If you want and need to find a well-maintained vehicle and you want to keep it that way, then please read on. I have said it before: The condition of a used car is basically an extension of the owner that previously owned the vehicle.

If you know the person who previously owned the car you are thinking of buying, that is a definite plus. Knowing the person who owned the vehicle, and also knowing that they serviced the car on a regular basis, with all of the service records available, is one of the best situations to be in. I also need to mention that it helps greatly if it is a one-owner vehicle, meaning that they purchased the car brand-new and did not drive it like a maniac!

One of my many goals in this book is to have you, the consumer, purchase a good, dependable used car that will last you for many years, even after you have paid it off. There is one catch. You have to set money aside each year to maintain it. You should expect to set aside $1200 to $1500 a year just to maintain your car properly. So are you up to it? Can you afford $4 to $5 a day to take good care of your car? You can afford to by a coffee in the morning or lunch in the afternoon, or you might throw money away on a lottery tickets—or worse yet, cigarettes. So come on! If you can spend money on those things, you can certainly afford to set aside $4 a day to take care of the car that gets you from point A to point B, can't you? Hopefully you agree with me on this subject because if not, you may be setting yourself up for disaster. You would not buy a house with every last penny you have and not set aside money in case your water heater or furnace failed would you? That is called being house poor. If you do not set funds aside to maintain or repair your car, you could easily become car poor! When people are buying a car, most think only about the monthly payment. They tend to forget about the cost of ownership, which includes registration, insurance, repairs, and general maintenance for their car. Please give it some serious thought and factor all of these costs in before you buy. Do not be foolish and let your emotions take over. Think.

If you are fortunate enough to open the glove box and find that the previous owner kept a log of all the services performed on the car, it's like hitting the jackpot! If your friend's Aunt Becky has a car for sale that she originally purchased brand-new and brought to the local garage, and they always did everything the car needed for service from day one, this may be the car for you. However, it may not be the car for you if there are no service records available to prove exactly what services or repairs were done, as well as when and why they were done. A lot of quick lube places will bedazzle you with 20-point, 30-point, or 50-point checks. You might not question if all points were done, especially if you got the inside of your car vacuumed! When I am retired one day and I am no longer servicing my own vehicles, I will be sure to have them serviced by a mechanic that takes their time. Remember that quicker is not always better.

My point here is that Aunt Becky may have brought her car in for service on a regular basis and had her oil and filter changed, and all fluid levels checked. Did they check the fluid levels and the CONDITION OF THE FLUIDS? Who knows? Maybe that is all Aunt Becky knew? Perhaps all she knew was to go in to get lube, oil, and filter changes. You must take into consideration that most mechanics get only thirty minutes tops to do an oil change, and if the mechanic is not looking at the car while the oil is draining, she is definitely not getting her money's worth!

Even if you go by what the owner's manual states for service intervals under normal conditions, it may not be enough. Every car is different, and everybody drives differently. The automotive manufacturer may state that you have to do very little to the car, in order to get you to buy the car. Low cost of ownership is one of the major selling points for a new car manufacturer.

A large portion of used vehicles that are found at a dealership or used car lot are purchased at auction. It has been my experience that if you are looking to find service records or even an owner's manual in the glove box of a car purchased at auction, good luck! You might find a lonely package of salt or ketchup from the drive-through! There are so many variables today when shopping for a good used car. The first thing you need to understand is that the certain someone who owned the used car may have gotten rid of it for a reason. Maybe they got rid of it because they could not afford the payment. If so, they probably could not afford to have it serviced, either.

Wouldn't it be great if that used car could talk to you and tell you exactly what it has been through during its lifespan? Now I know it may sound weird to have this approach, but what would you ask the car? You might ask it: "Were you ever in an accident? Did the person who owned you change your oil? If so, how often?" If you have the opportunity, actually ask the previous owner what they did or did not do to the car while they owned it. They might tell you what they did to the car when they owned the car, but how do you know for sure? Ask for service records if they are available. If they do not have them, ask where they took the car to have it serviced, and confirm with the service facility that they have the records.

We know that it is not possible for that used car to talk to us. I want this book to give you a great advantage when looking for a good, dependable used car. One day you may be driving past one of your local dealerships and a car may catch your eye. You may pull into the used car lot to take a closer look at the vehicle. You may ask yourself, "Where did this car come from? Who owned it?" I can tell you that there is a very good chance that it came from an auction. You will find that a good portion of used vehicles come from auction. The scary thing about this is that you do not know why it was sent to an auction in the first place. More often than not, a car that was sent to auction has a problem with it. If the dealership has a good auction buyer who knows what to look for, it may be an okay car.

Not all cars that come from auction are bad cars. If the car you may be interested in came from an auction and has 25,000 or less on it for mileage, you should consider it. I would seriously recommend an extended warranty on the car if it is offered to you. If a warranty is not offered to you, ask for one. The expense of an extended warranty will vary depending on the make and model of vehicle that you are interested in. The age and mileage will also directly affect the cost of the warranty. Be sure whenever possible to purchase a warranty offered by the automotive manufacturer—GM, Ford, Honda, Toyota, etc. The automotive manufacturer is more likely to stand behind what they offer for coverage, as opposed to an after-market warranty company.

When a salesperson wanders out to greet you when you are looking at the car, ask if the car came from auction. Make sure you make eye contact with the salesperson when you ask this question. If you are really interested in the car, call the dealership later on and ask a different salesperson or sales manager if the car came from auction. If you get two different answers, they have failed the trust-worthiness test. How do you know where the car came from? The truth is, if they are unable to tell you who previously owned the car, it likely came from auction.

Once when I worked at a dealership, one of the drivers drove a car back from an auction from Connecticut to New Hampshire. The service manager I worked with at the time told me that the driver who brought the car to us stated that he smelled the odor of burning wood coming from the front end of the vehicle. I did not give the comment too much thought, until I inspected the front brakes. Believe it or not, someone got handy with a band saw and made a set of brake pads out of wood to get the car to auction! At least they used hardwood to make the brake pads—how thoughtful! To this day, I do not know where the car came from before it went to auction. A person who makes wooden brake pads, and actually installs them into a vehicle, should be put in jail, NO QUESTIONS ASKED!

Formerly leased cars are typically turned in between 20,000 and 30,000 miles. Historically, people who have leased these vehicles have done the absolute bare minimum to the cars to maintain them. Why, you ask? Because the car is not actually owned by the person. Let's face it, when you rent a car you do not actually care about the car, do you? You must have heard stories about someone renting a car and abusing it, haven't you? All a leased vehicle is, in my opinion, is a car that has basically been rented for two years or so. Not all leased cars are bad; you just have to know what to look and listen for.

I have recommended maintenance to people who are leasing a car, and have been shot down almost every time because they do not actually own the car. Most people who lease a vehicle do try to maintain their leased vehicle, but not at the same level as someone who owns a vehicle outright. When a leased vehicle is turned in, it is not usually checked over very closely. The tires may be looked at, or a visual inspection of the body for damage may be done. Of course the mileage is noted to make sure you did not go over the allowed mileage. Most of the time, when someone leases a car they will turn around and do it again. If this is the case, then you must understand that the salesman is not going to be so inspired to check over the car you just turned in. He or she is focused on getting you into another leased car, ASAP!

I am not saying that all formerly leased cars are bad cars, but it does make a difference if a dealer has its act together, meaning the vehicle was checked over well, and its maintenance was brought up to date before it was put on the lot to be sold. What it basically boils down to is this: The mechanic needs to check over the previously used or leased vehicle and find things that it needs so he can get a paycheck. The car salesman is hoping that the mechanic who looks the car over does not find too much wrong with the car, so it does not cut into his profit margin. It has been, is, and always will be this way.

Whether this is your first car or your tenth car, take the time to be methodical in your search, and it will pay off. The ideal situation to be in when buying a used car is to know the person who owned the car, preferably a family member. Find a vehicle that will suit your needs. Be practical if need be. Just remember, if it's the first car you are looking at buying, take the time to make sure it's the right one for you. The memory of your first car may stay with you for the rest of your life!

CHAPTER 2
The Previous Owner

How many times have you seen it? You are driving down the road, minding your own business, and all of a sudden you look in the rearview mirror and somebody is riding your tail. I mean, you can barely even see their headlights in your rearview mirror because they are so close to you. That is way too close! Let me ask you this: Why are they riding your tail? Because they did not allow themselves enough time to get out the door that particular morning—or quite possibly they do that every morning. Do you think they allow the car to warm up? I am willing to bet you they turned the key, started the car, shifted it into gear, took off quickly, and got to work late anyway.

Everybody has done it. You wake up late and you rush out of the house to get to work on time. As soon as your car's engine starts, you throw it in gear and take off down the road. It won't hurt your car too much to do this every now and again, but if you were to do this every day, you might end up paying for it sooner than you would like to. Just imagine, by comparison, if your alarm went off, you jumped out of bed naked, and ran outside without any shoes on to go to work every day! You would not have a very good life, would you? Now how do you think your car would feel about that if it could talk to you? Not too good, I would imagine. You will not find too many used cars out there this day in age that have not been exposed to this type of abuse, and more. It seems everyone is in a hurry today.

Would you be interested in buying a used car that was not warmed up every morning? Maybe, or maybe not. This is most important in colder climates. Today's motor oils are formulated to protect most engine components on cold start, but it is most important to let your car's engine warm up for least two to three minutes. The most damage can be done to your engine when first starting it. It is important to let it run for a while before taking off, to contribute to a long engine lifespan—not to mention the automatic transmission. It is just as important to allow the automatic transmission to warm up as well. Automatic transmission fluid needs to warm up so it can flow properly through the vast network of passages.

You can tell who does not allow for warm-up time. Have you ever had someone pull out in front of you first thing on a cold morning and you notice a big white smoke cloud coming out of their tailpipe? Did you notice the smell? This means that they did not allow proper warm-up time for their car. Under heavy acceleration, exhaust pressure is pushing out condensation that has built up overnight. The catalytic converter is not hot enough to function properly, and that is why there is odor from the exhaust. No need to panic; if you see a small white cloud coming out of your car when you first start it in the morning, in most cases this can be considered normal. The only time it is not normal is if it smells sweet. This would indicate your vehicle's engine is burning antifreeze. The problem should be addressed as soon as possible, especially if the smoke does not stop after your car is fully warmed up. Your engine's antifreeze/coolant is engineered to remove heat efficiently from your engine, as well as protect it from freezing in the winter. What do you think the chances are that someone who is constantly in a hurry will change their antifreeze/coolant when they should?

If you have the opportunity to ask the previous owner if they allowed their car to warm up for a while before taking off, by all means ask them. You must understand, however, that you should not let your car idle for too long. Your car is designed to be moving most of the time while it is running. It is not a good habit to get into letting your car idle for extended amounts of time, especially in the hot summer months if you are stuck in traffic. If your engine's cooling fan is not functioning, it may be a good idea for you to turn your engine off for a while, until you can resume driving. This just might stop your engine from overheating to the point of causing severe engine damage. Always try to keep one eye on your temperature gauge, to see that it is staying just below the halfway point. In cases such as this, synthetic oil can help protect your engine from overheating in certain situations.

Years ago, Mobil 1 aired a commercial that featured conventional motor oil poured into a frying pan. It quickly burned from the excessive heat. They did the same thing with a frying pan next to it, at the same extreme temperature, with their Mobil 1 synthetic oil.

It did not burn. Synthetic oil is a good investment, especially if you are exposing your car's engine to all types of extremes. If you can find a used car that has had synthetic oil used in it from day one, and it was changed regularly, you may have hit yourself a home run.

Service records, service records, service records! At times it may seem as if I am repeating myself in this book. I want to make sure I am getting my point across to you. One of the most important questions that you need to ask the person or the dealership is: "Do you have the service records for this used vehicle?"

Sure, the person who owned this car probably took really good care of the car, especially if they bought it brand-new. However, as time goes by, usually the last couple years that a person owns a car, they tend to let things go. Maybe they just let the oil change go overdue by two or three thousand miles. Or, let's say, a rattle or a new noise will pop up out of nowhere and they just turn the radio up a little louder, trying to put that noise out of their mind. They don't plan on keeping the car for much longer anyway. Searching for a good, dependable used car is hard enough, let alone trying to find the previous owner of the car, when purchasing from a dealership. It is important that you do your homework. In most cases, the last year that someone owns a vehicle could quite possibly be the worst year of the car's life! This is where their problem becomes your problem, if you buy the vehicle.

You may never be able to find the previous owner of a car you are thinking about purchasing, especially if it came from an auction. Many vehicles that fell victim to Hurricane Katrina made their way up north to be sold. Many of these vehicles were flood vehicles and were exposed to bacteria-infested water. These vehicles were marked biohazard and were not supposed to be resold to the public. These cars were designated to be scrapped and salvaged. However, these vehicles sat for such a long time that any stickers or markings that indicated they were a biohazard either peeled off or faded away. If you hear someone has gotten a really good deal on a used car that came from the South, or a vehicle that has been exposed to flood damage or worse, buyer beware!

If the potential used car you may purchase seems to smell really good inside, they may have covered it up with Carpet Fresh or some other form of deodorizer. Keep in mind that this pretty smell may be covering up something such as cigarette smoke, or dog. As time goes by, the pretty smell will wear off and the smell that they were trying to cover up will shine through … surprise! A very similar thing happened to my wife when she purchased a used 2005 Honda Pilot. The people we purchased the vehicle from really did a decent job cleaning up the Pilot; however, we later found out that the woman had smoked. After three weeks, the nicotine- and smoke-permeated cloth seats and headliner started to smell like cigarette smoke again.

I used an ionizer to try and rid the vehicle of the old cigarette smoke smell twice. It did not work. It was okay for about a month each time that I did this, but the smell returned again! The only way I got rid of the cigarette smell was to shampoo the entire interior of the car. I mean the headliner, seats, carpet, and sun visors. You name it; if it was made of cloth, it got shampooed. This was the only way to completely get rid of the cigarette smell. We did not think to ask the previous owner if she smoked or not. We wish we had, because we might not have purchased the vehicle had we known it was smoked in. You may not have to ask the person you buy the vehicle from if they smoke, because it may be a dead giveaway if you see cigarette burns on the seat or anywhere else inside the vehicle. This may be information that you don't really need. Maybe you don't want to know what the inside of the car looked and smelled like before it was cleaned, but this is where it can be very helpful if you know the previous owner.

If you are thinking of purchasing a used car from a dealership, you may want to ask the salesperson what their policy is regarding odors that appear a few weeks after purchase. If it starts to smell like the previous owner's bad habits, they may offer to professionally clean the vehicle again at no charge. Get it in writing, or you may be cleaning the car yourself or paying someone else to professionally clean the car.

Clean car, one owner!

Here is a previous owner story for you. A customer came to the shop I work in with a Pontiac Aztec. This one was bright yellow. You would not have any trouble being seen in this vehicle, for sure! Shortly after the customer purchased this used vehicle from a Ford dealership in the area, the vehicle developed an overheating condition. Our shop foreman diagnosed the vehicle as needing head gaskets. This was a pretty big job and a hard pill to swallow, especially after purchasing the vehicle without a used car warranty. After about $1200 worth of work, the vehicle was fixed. The customer paid their bill and they were on their way, back on the road. Ten thousand miles later, the vehicle developed this overheating condition again. We drained the cooling system down and replaced the thermostat again, just to rule out that the new one might be sticking, causing the engine to overheat. We refilled the cooling system and bled all the air out of the system, to make sure that the cooling fans worked as they should—and they did. A ten-mile road test confirmed that the vehicle was fine.

The customer drove the vehicle for approximately another forty miles. It was returned to our shop with a customer complaint that the engine was again overheating. At this point in time the vehicle gave every indication that air was entering into the cooling system, causing the vehicle to overheat. With new head gaskets on the vehicle, we suspected that one of the cylinder heads had a crack, causing air to enter into the cooling system from the combustion chambers. We informed the customer of the situation—this time the job could possibly cost over $2,500. The customer decided not to invest the money into the vehicle again. They decided to have us fill the cooling system, so they could drive it to the Ford dealership and trade it in for another vehicle.

Clearly this Pontiac Aztec was a lemon. The customer took this used vehicle back to the dealer they bought it from. This vehicle would have been a great candidate for an extended warranty. The customer did not inform the dealership of the overheating issue with the vehicle, nor did they intend to. Is this right? Not exactly—however, they did feel like they had been taken, purchasing this Pontiac Aztec. From a moral standpoint this is wrong, especially for the next person who may consider buying this vehicle. Hopefully, the next person to purchase this Pontiac Aztec will buy an extended warranty. It is not likely that this vehicle went back out onto the lot. It is likely that the vehicle was sent to auction.

Unfortunately, this kind of thing happens all the time, when people own a car for a short or a long time and they just cannot afford to invest another penny into their vehicle. Can you really blame them? This is why you have to be so careful when you buy a used car. After you read this book, hopefully it will keep you on your toes, so you won't get taken by a bad used car deal.

It is not a bad idea to stick your nose into a *Consumer Reports* magazine and read about the reliability of the particular vehicle you are thinking of buying. You can also access the worldwide web and look for forums that relate to the vehicle that you are thinking of purchasing. If you're thinking about trading your old car and you know it has a problem, be careful, because what goes around comes around!

Years ago a co-worker had a chance to buy a 1989 Honda Civic. An older gentleman had decided that it was time for him to turn his driver's license in and sell his car. The car had very low mileage. This can be good and bad. The good news was that the former owner serviced the vehicle regularly and it had only about 30,000 miles on it. The problem was that the vehicle sat a lot more than he drove the car. His wife had passed away years ago, so he mainly drove where he had to go, usually alone. With that in mind, nobody really used any of the other window switches or door lock switches.

After my co-worker purchased the car, he went to take his two boys for a ride to the store. His son said, "Hey, Dad—how come I can't get my door open?" So Dad went around to the passenger's side door to see what he was talking about. Sure enough, the door hinges were so badly seized up from lack of use that he could barely open the door himself. The same condition applied to the rear doors. He went back into the house, grabbed a can of WD-40, and generously sprayed the hinges and the door checks until the doors operated fairly well.

They continued on with their trip to the store. It was a nice day and his son decided he wanted to put the window down. He asked his father, "Hey, Dad—how come my window switch does not work?"

He replied, "Well, it should work!" So they finally pulled into the store parking lot and he went to the other side of the car and examined the window switch. Lack of use had caused the switch to seize in the center position. Later on, he had to remove the switches and free them up as best as he could. The vehicle had other issues with dry rotting rubber components, not to mention the tires. This is why you have to be careful with an older vehicle with low miles. These items were easily addressed, but they were surprises.

When I worked at a Honda dealership, our general manager at the time was raving about how he basically stole this Honda Pilot EX from the auction. They had a lot of room for profit, since they purchased it cheap. The only thing he said that needed to be addressed was that the check engine light was on. The service department needed to check what the trouble code was in the vehicle's computer. I hooked up the scan tool and found that the Pilot had #2 and #3 cylinder misfires. This seemed a little odd for this vehicle, with only around 60,000 miles on it. The Pilot had leaking exhaust valves in #2 and #3 cylinders. Even after checking, the excessive valve clearances indicated that the valves were bent, and I had to tear down the engine to repair it. Now keep in mind, I was in the diagnostic detective mode. The vehicle could not tell me what had happened to it, but coming from the auction, it was anyone's guess.

What we found were bent exhaust valves in #2 and #3 cylinders. How did they get bent, you ask? We found out that the Pilot was originally purchased in New York. Early production Honda Pilots and Odysseys had problems with the hydraulic tensioners—that's the part that keeps the engine's timing belt tight. These tensioners had a safety recall on them and would be replaced at no charge to the customer. In this case, we suspected that the customer who owned the vehicle originally may have received the recall notice, but not paid attention to it. They thought it was junk mail and threw the recall notice in the trash, which resulted in never getting the tensioner replaced. It then failed, causing engine damage.

Apparently, the dealer in New York took the engine apart and replaced only the valves that were visually bent, and threw the engine back together. The engine's #2 and #3 cylinder valves should have been replaced, but they were not. Honda supposedly had to buy the vehicle back. Somehow the Pilot got sent to an auction with this ailment. We were the lucky ones to get it. I replaced all of the valves in this engine, reassembled it, and it was fine after that. Honda was reluctant to pay for the work that I had done on the Pilot, because it was a buy-back vehicle. Honda had already paid a warranty claim for the poor work done at the previous Honda dealership. *What is the moral of this story? Always have the used vehicle you are thinking of purchasing checked for any open recalls from the manufacturer!*

The current auto repair shop that I am working at now has a small sales department. The salesperson, Eric, told me a story about a customer who traded in their car. This customer had dogs, and the dogs went everywhere with them in their car. The car did have an odor from the dogs, and a good reconditioning would take care of the smell. The customer had removed all the items from the car and handed the keys to Eric. He shut the doors and locked the vehicle. Eric made plans to have the vehicle cleaned in a couple of days. A couple of days passed, and Eric handed the keys to the reconditioning guy. Eric said, "Shampoo this vehicle; it smells like dog. I need to get it cleaned so we can sell this vehicle easier."

The young man took the keys from Eric and got into the car to bring it to his wash bay, only to find that the vehicle was infested with fleas, and so was he! What happened here? The owner cleaned all of the belongings out of the car, but they left their dogs' fleas behind! Eric informed me that the remaining fleas in the vehicle were closed up tight. When this happens, the fleas basically have nowhere to go—in other words, they panic, and breed like crazy! If the windows had been left open, the fleas would have escaped and not infested the vehicle.

The next time you go shopping and you are walking through the parking lot, glance at the inside of some of the vehicles as you pass by them. By doing this, you can get a really good idea as to how some people do not take care of their vehicles. You may quickly see that most vehicles may resemble what might look like the inside of a full dumpster! Hopefully, I don't sound too critical by mentioning this, but in today's fast-paced society many people do not have the time to keep their cars clean or properly maintained. Just think, most of those cars could be traded in, reconditioned, and put on a used car lot for a full retail price. You could be the next person in line to purchase a vehicle ... think about it.

You can expect surprises when you are searching for a used vehicle. Be aware that there are many more surprises out there than I have mentioned—that's for sure!

CHAPTER 3
Searching for the Right Vehicle

The three most important points when searching for a vehicle are cost of ownership, resale value, and reliability. First, cost of ownership is important for the obvious reasons. You want to be careful with cost of ownership because the manufacturer of the vehicle will tell you what you want to hear. How much is the car you are interested in buying going to cost you per year for maintenance and repairs? Ask somebody who drives a car that is similar to what you want to purchase. Or call an automotive service department that services that vehicle and get some examples of typical repair bills, etc. Secondly, how well will your car hold its value after you buy it? And finally, think about reliability. Make sure to look around online for reviews and reliability reports about the car you may want to purchase. THIS IS VERY IMPORTANT!

What do I drive? As I am writing this book, I drive a Toyota Tundra and my wife drives a Honda Pilot. Both vehicles are made in the USA by Americans. It amazes me that so many people do not realize that most of these vehicles are built by the American people. Both vehicles have a good resale value and are dependable to boot—very dependable. Please do not base your decision on what I drive. My choices as a mechanic are based on what is not towed into the shop on a regular basis. I am exposed every day to which vehicles are breaking down on the road. Make sure you do your homework, give yourself time, and base your decision on your findings. Information is everywhere on the internet. I suggest that you use it to your full advantage—you won't regret it.

So where do you start? *Consumer Reports* prints a great magazine every year that informs you of the best and worst new and used vehicles. I highly recommend you pick one up as a starting point. *Consumer Reports* has a simple, easy-to-understand rating system. This is a great advantage for you when looking for a used car. Then, you can surf your local dealership's used car inventory area on the internet. Then do a drive-through. We are in the information age, that is for sure, and if you allow yourself the time you will find the perfect car. One of the best places to start is on the worldwide web. Start with Google, J.D Power, Consumer Reports, Kelley Blue Book. com, Edmunds.com, etc.

How old should a used car be? If it is within your budget, you should consider buying a used vehicle that is about two to three years old—with available service records, of course. Also, with about

20,000 to 30,000 miles on it, this age and mileage is your best option for a dependable used car.

You will pay more for a used vehicle at a dealership than you will if you buy a private sale used vehicle. You have to do your homework and be patient. You could very well save yourself $3,000-$5,000 by not paying that so-called retail starting price. If you decide to buy from a dealer, in most cases, you can get a warranty or return the vehicle within 30 days, if the car has problems that are too expensive to fix. Remember, however, that the $3,000 to $5,000 you might save by purchasing a private sale car may be spent on repairs in the near future, so it's about due diligence on your part. If you buy the private sale car, you will be buying the car typically on an "as-is, asseen" basis. In that case, you are married to the car. *Keep in mind you can purchase an after-market warranty for your used car. Just make doubly sure you know exactly what is covered.* I strongly recommend you purchase a warranty from a reputable dealership. The price of the extended warranty will depend on the make, model, and year of the vehicle. In other words, you will pay less on a warranty for a vehicle that has a good track record, and more for one that does not.

On an internet search Auto Trader.com and Craigslist.com are great places to find private-sale cars. Remember, if you find a car you are interested in on the internet, never have them bring the car to your home! Make sure you meet the person in a public place during the daytime, and take a friend along with you when possible. If you find a car halfway across the country, and the seller states they will ship the car to you, don't fall for that. There is a good chance for you to get ripped off.

You can even look on eBay or the trusty classifieds section in your local newspaper. All the choices you have today can be confusing, especially if you need a new car yesterday. Hopefully, you do have time to be methodical in your search to find the right car for yourself and your family. Think for a moment about the car you have right now. What do you like about the car? Is the car too big or too small for your needs? Is it a gas hog?

Toyota has the best advertisement: "Ask somebody who owns one!" This is true for any car out there. Don't be afraid to approach someone loading groceries in their car and say, "Hi there, I'm thinking about purchasing a Volkswagen. How has it treated you? What is your annual cost of ownership to own and maintain your car?" Maybe that would be too bold a question to ask a perfect stranger— how much it costs to own their car. Chances are they may not be able to give you an exact number off the cuff anyway. Obviously, you would not rest your decision on this one encounter, but in the early stages of finding a dependable car, it's a good start. The best advice that I can give you is to call a dealership's service department and give the make and model of the vehicle you are thinking of purchasing. Ask them what a typical annual cost of ownership for that particular vehicle may be per year.

You need to write down on paper exactly what you want in your next vehicle, and what you can afford to spend. I strongly recommend that you start by doing the drive-through at a dealership on a Sunday. This way you can actually get out and look at the vehicle without getting bombarded by salespeople. I suggest that you take a slow walk around the car looking for paint overspray under the wheel wells. Look for mismatched paint as well. Kneel down to the rear of the car and look closely down both sides of the car. You might be surprised at what you see! You should not see any waves down the side of the vehicle's exterior body panels. You can also spot dents that you may not see looking at the car straight on. The best way to find defects on a vehicle's paint is to wash the car. You wouldn't believe what you can see when you get up close and personal like that with a car. Now, it might seem weird if you ask a salesman if you can wash the car yourself before you buy it. You at least want to kneel down and look closely at the paint and body panels.

The first time you wash your car, you will notice imperfections or small dents in the body, especially if you wax it. Keep in mind that it is a used car and it will not be perfect. The shop that I am employed with now has a body shop. When the body repairman is done with his work, he washes the car himself, to see if he can locate any imperfections in his work. This can be an advantage when making your decision to buy or not to buy.

Look underneath the car for fluid loss such as engine oil, transmission fluid, and engine coolant. Don't kick the tires—salespeople do not like tire kickers. If you think you may be interested in the vehicle, make sure to write down the stock number or the serial number. It can be hard to peek through the window and get the mileage of the vehicle, since most cars have digital odometers these days. You can call the dealership the next day to get the vehicle mileage. This way you can go on Kelley Blue Book.com and see what retail may be on the vehicle that you are interested in. This will give you some extra leverage to get a fair price on the car. Some dealerships will already have the Kelley Blue Book price printed out for you in the car. Be prepared! A seasoned salesperson these days is expecting you to wave the Kelley Blue Book in their face. If you are

trading your old car in and you tell them that Kelley Blue Book states your car is worth $3,800, be prepared to be insulted. They may say that those numbers are not valid, and they can give you only $500 for your car! Or they may tell you the car you want to trade it in for is priced well below retail, and that is why they are unable to give you $3,800 for your car. Don't believe that, either! If you find yourself in this situation, you should turn and walk away. Try your car on your own.

Used cars can be marked up at a dealership from $2000-$4000 over what they actually paid for the car. To give you some idea, when you are on Kelley Blue Book.com, see what the trade-in value is on the car. This will give you some idea of what they paid for the car. What is an honest profit that a dealership should make on the sale of a used car? Keep in mind that they have to put some money into the car to get a retail price for it, including reconditioning, and passing a safety inspection. Honestly, I believe that $800 to $1,000 should be considered an honest profit per dealership or used car facility on a vehicle. That is after the cost of what they put into the car to get it out on the lot.

Do you have a friend who has dealt with a certain salesperson and had a good experience with them? In this case, you should have your friend get a business card from the salesperson. This way, if you buy a car from him or her, your friend may get a $50 bird dog fee! It's always nice to have a little extra unexpected grocery money. If you are really interested in a certain vehicle at a dealership and you have got a salesperson in mind, give him or her a phone call and ask a few questions about the car. Do not let them know just how interested you are in the car. A good salesperson can smell your interest in the car over the phone! Just ask a few simple questions about the car, such as: How many miles are on the car? Was it a one-owner car? Are there any service records for the car? Also, you want to ask if they have CARFAX information on the vehicle. What is CARFAX? CARFAX.com is a website where for a nominal fee you can get a vehicle history report. Most reputable dealerships will already have all of this information ready for you. Let the salesperson know which car you are interested in, and that you would like to come in for a test drive.

Don't be afraid to ask the salesperson to go out and put a hold tag on the car, because someone could be looking at the car as you are talking to the salesperson on the phone. On many occasions I have talked to people who wished they'd had a hold tag put on a car they were interested in, and did not. The car was snatched away from them! Also, last but not least, if you are thinking about trading your old car, do not let the salesperson know until he has first given you some numbers in writing. If the salesperson asks, "So, will you be trading your current vehicle?" you don't have to give a direct answer; just say you're undecided, and you may sell it outright. Then you can change the subject and ask, "How about a test drive? When can I come in?" The salesperson will more than likely say you can come in anytime, of course. Before you go to the dealership, make sure your current car is as clean as possible. Yes, you did just say that you might sell your car outright, but then again, you may not sell it to your neighbor. The first impression of your old car will be a lasting one to the salesperson whom you are dealing with. It may be well worth your time to clean the old car up a little bit!

Ironically, in the process of writing this book, I was in a search for a new truck—not a brand spanking new truck, but new to me, of course; the old 1997 Ford F150 had almost 150,000 miles and I'd had it for nearly nine years. It was time for a change—and yes, I had all the service receipts and records for the person I sold it to.

One night my wife Melinda was looking in the classifieds. She read to me as follows: "2005 Tundra; 40,000 miles; perfectly maintained; $19,900." This did catch my interest. I checked Kelley Blue Book and the retail is $24,000 for the truck. I wrote down all my questions for the seller, and I made the phone call. The guy who owned the truck was a carpenter. He seemed like a very nice guy. I had many questions for him, and he answered almost all of my questions. He said he had purchased the truck new and changed the engine oil and filter every 3,000 miles. He told me that he was basically obsessed with taking care of the truck. He said his wife made fun of him because he kept a towel on the driver's seat, to keep the seat looking like new. After about fifteen minutes of questions, I decided that the truck might be what I was looking for.

I decided to stop torturing him with a million questions, and made arrangements to see the truck. He lived five miles from where my wife works, so we met him at her office parking lot. He showed up in the parking lot with the Toyota Tundra. It was a beautiful summer day. The truck was a wonderful deep sapphire blue. Later, I found the color to be called Spectra Mica. I introduced myself to him and we shook hands. I immediately went over the vehicle with a fine tooth comb. From a distance the truck was perfect, but close up I saw some small dings and scratches. I could also see that the paint on the truck had never been waxed, as far as I could tell.

The truck was going to need tires soon, but for now they passed inspection. I was going to need new tires for the truck before winter that was for sure! Let's take a look inside the vehicle. Was there a towel on the driver's seat? Yes, there was! Was there a plastic bag covering the back of the passenger's side seat back to prevent his six-year-old from staining the seat? Sure was! Was this guy neat freak that I thought he was, when we talked on the phone? Almost. The console was packed with loose change and lots of rubber bands. His children's dirty socks and toys were strewn about the interior of the truck. The windows were dirty. He had CD cases everywhere with no CDs. The CDs were everywhere on the floor of the vehicle. Do I need to mention the rock-hard McDonald's French fries poking out from under the seat? He was obviously a busy guy and did not have the time to clean his truck before showing it to me. That was okay, because I knew it would clean up easily. Now it was time to take a look under the hood.

I popped the hood open, and just as I kind of expected, the top of the battery was filthy with corrosion, kind of resembling the surface of the moon. The engine oil was low about one quart, the antifreeze reservoir was nearly empty, and the air filter was dirty. This was not entirely his fault; he was paying someone to do this for him, and he was not really getting his money's worth from what I could see. I asked him who he had serviced the vehicle. He told me an independent shop in town, and sometimes the dealer serviced the vehicle. I told him that sometimes it pays to open the hood to see what you just paid for. He told me he shouldn't have to do that because he is paying them to do that! I quickly agreed with him, but made him aware that to find a good shop, sometimes you have to do that to know for sure what you just paid for. Remember, it takes only one shoddy mechanic to make a good shop look bad. Find a good mechanic and don't be afraid to ask for him or her by name when you call and schedule your next service appointment. He asked me what I thought about the truck.

I replied, "To be totally honest with you, I am a little disappointed with your presentation of the vehicle. It's kind of dirty on the outside and there is a lot of clutter on the inside."

He replied, "I did not want you to think I had anything to hide from you." In that way I had to admire his honesty, and I did end up buying the truck, as you know. We became friends and still are to this day.

In the previous chapter, I shared with you the experience that my wife and I had purchasing her 2005 Honda Pilot. Also in this chapter, sharing my recent experience searching for and finding my Toyota Tundra can give you insight into the process of choosing a good used vehicle. There are many choices you can make when trying to locate a good used vehicle. Use the internet, classifieds, and word-of-mouth from people you know. Ultimately, I want this book to be a reference point in locating the vehicle that meets your wants and needs. Most importantly, take your time in your search, and it will pay off. Don't be impulsive, because it could bite you!

CHAPTER 4
Knowing What to Look and Listen for Under the Hood

This vehicle's hood on the left has been replaced. Notice the stickers or labels are missing under the hood. Note vehicle's hood on the right; stickers are intact and this hood is original.

Knowing what to look for and listen for underneath the hood of an automobile is a very important step. I'm not just talking about the engine. It's important to look at the underside of the hood to make sure all emission stickers and VIN tags are in their proper places. As you can see, the car on the left has been in a wreck. Its engine hood has been replaced and the emission stickers were not replaced. If the stickers or tags are not in their proper position or missing, this could indicate that the vehicle has had some collision work in the past. You also need to know that the engine and transmission should have VIN tags on them that match the tags on the vehicle's fenders and doors.

Engine VIN tag shown above

If the tags on the engine and transmission do not match the numbers and letters on the body panels, this means that the transmission or the engine has been replaced. Many times if a vehicle's hood has been replaced, the body shop will neglect to replace the stickers. This is a dead giveaway indicating that the vehicle has had collision work done. Also, you need to know that not all auto manufacturers use vehicle identification tags on their body panels, but many do use them. Look at the bolts that secure the fenders and make sure that there are no signs of missing paint from them, indicating that the fender has been either taken off or replaced in the past.

The engine on the left only has 60K miles on it and has been neglected. The engine on the right has 89K miles on it and has seen regular scheduled services.

Now, let's take a look inside the engine. I want you to unscrew the engine oil cover. This is where you fill the engine with oil. Once you get the oil cover off, look at the inside of the cover. You should not see any signs of sludge. The engine pictured above on right has 89k miles on it and has seen regular oil changes. Depending on the valve cover design, you may not be able to see too much inside the engine. It helps to bring along a small flashlight to help you see inside the engine a little bit better, after you have removed the engine oil cap. The inside of the engine's components should have a light brown color with no signs of black sludge inside the engine. Any aluminum components should still appear light in color, or a light brown color. If you do notice a lot of black sludge in the engine, you may notice oil leaks from the engine.

In figure above on the left, you can see, with the oil cap removed, the black sludge inside the engine. This vehicle has around 60K miles on its engine and does not see regular maintenance. When you see this black sludge, you will not likely see service records to go with it. Most oil leaks can be caused from lack of oil changes. This lack of oil changes over time hardens the seals, so they cannot seal as they were designed to do.

Lack of oil changes ruined the seals in
this engine, among other things.

This is another reason why it is important to gather as much information about the vehicle as you can before you actually make the decision to purchase. If there is a car you're interested in at a dealership, ask the salesperson where the car may have came from. If the vehicle was traded in by somebody locally, ask the salesperson for that information. The salesperson may not disclose that information to you. Or the salesperson may not let you know if the car came from an auction or not. In any case, early in the process just let the salesperson know that this will be the difference between your buying the car and not buying the car. If you are able to contact the previous owner, you may be able to find out a lot of things about the car when they owned it. Some questions you could ask them include: Why did you get rid of the car? Had the car ever been in an accident, or did it have any major collision work? Did you service the vehicle regularly? Hopefully, you are able to gather as much of this information as possible, because it can be very valuable for you in the future. It can also give you great leverage when you are ready to make a deal with the salesperson.

Now take your flashlight and look closely at the radiator. See if you can notice any signs of leakage. The best spots to find leakage in the radiator are at the upper and lower radiator covers. Sometimes you can see leakage where the covers meet the radiator seals. Over time they can start to leak. A radiator can also show signs of leakage at the core area of the radiator. You may not see signs of actual antifreeze; you may, however, see a crusty substance forming at the sealing areas of the radiator or radiator hoses. This can give a clear indication of a slow antifreeze leak. This may also be noticed at the head gasket area, indicating the start of a small antifreeze leak. In this case, if you do see any leakages at the cylinder head gasket area, you may want to shut the hood of the car and keep on looking. A head gasket leak will be hard for the untrained eye to find, especially if it is an internal leak, so you would need to get the opinion from your mechanic if this is in question.

You can basically check every hose under the hood that carries antifreeze and examine them closely for leakage. Pay close attention to the hose clamps. You may see a hose clamp that has been over-tightened with someone's effort to not have a coolant leak, but in turn, they have caused a coolant leak by over-tightening the hose clamp. Usually this means that the radiator hose has been damaged and will need to be replaced to correct the leak. Make sure the coolant hoses show no signs of bulging, or ballooning.

Note crusty substance—this is dried coolant
on this reservoir line, indicating a leak.

Take a look at the engine's external drive belts. Make sure that there is no sign of cracking on the inside surface of the belts. When the car is first started, you may hear the belts chirping—this condition is even a better reason to look closely at the belts. One portion of the belt may look fine, and another portion may have cracks. Any belts that show signs of cracking should be replaced as soon as possible to ensure reliability.

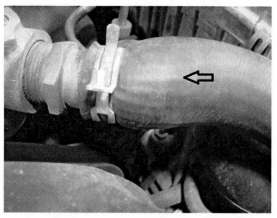

This radiator hose was ready to rupture!
Replaced in the nick of time!

This serpentine belt is badly cracked and well overdue for replacement.

Another belt to be very concerned about is the engine's timing belt. If equipped, it is very important that this belt is up-to-date. This belt connects the bottom of the engine to the top of the engine. If and when this belt snaps, it can cause serious engine damage, greatly reducing the weight of your wallet! The only real way to examine this belt is to remove the old belt, bend it backward, and check it for cracks. However, if you were to remove the belt just to examine it, you would replace it anyway, with the amount of labor that it would take just to inspect the belt.

This badly cracked timing belt was replaced in
the nick of time!

This is an example of a timing chain in a
well-taken-care-of engine.

Sometimes you can see cracks on the outside of the belt, but you don't usually see this indication. If the vehicle you may potentially purchase does not have records of the timing belt ever being replaced, once purchased, it would be wise to replace it, for peace of mind. Any good mechanic will write on the sticker provided with the new timing belt the mileage and date that the belt was replaced. Usually, the sticker is applied to the top timing belt cover. How do you tell if an engine has a timing belt or a timing chain? One way to tell is that most engines use a plastic cover to enclose the timing belt.

Call any automotive dealer and ask them if the particular vehicle that you are interested in buying has an interference or freewheeling engine. If they tell you that the engine has a freewheeling engine, it means that if the timing belt fails, the engine should not sustain any engine damage. If they tell you that the engine has an interference engine, it means if the timing belt fails, there is most likely going to be major engine damage as a result.

Another component I strongly recommend you replace, when replacing the timing belt, is the engine's water pump, especially if the water pump is driven by the timing belt. It may cost you an additional half an hour or so in labor cost, plus the added cost of the water pump, but it is worth it in the long run to replace this pump. There is no way that an old water pump will last as long as the new timing belt that was just replaced. If you replace just the timing belt, you will more than likely have to replace the water pump midway through the lifespan of the timing belt you just replaced.

One of two things usually happens when a water pump starts to fail. Most times, a good mechanic will notice a small loss of coolant leaking from the old water pump, or may notice abnormal noise due to worn bearings in the water pump. One of the worst things that can happen is that the noisy water pump bearings go unnoticed and the water pump seizes, causing timing belt failure, and quite possibly severe engine damage. Many of today's vehicles use a hydraulic tensioner to keep the engine's timing belt properly tensioned. In this case it is very important that you replace this tensioner along with the water pump. Usually, the hydraulic tensioner will show signs of oil leakage. It would be foolish not to replace the hydraulic tensioner, because it is not likely this tensioner will outlast the new timing belt or water pump.

If the engine has a timing chain that connects the bottom end of the engine to the top end of the engine, you really have nothing to worry about—unless, of course, the engine has not seen regular oil changes. This causes premature wear of the timing chain, gears, and components. Often a timing chain will give you some warning if it is going to fail; this is usually indicated by a rattling-type noise from the front of the engine. Timing chain replacement usually requires much more labor to replace the chain gear set and tensioner than it does to replace a timing belt. If an engine's timing chain needs to be replaced, the rest of the engine—and the whole car, for that matter—may need to be carefully evaluated.

There could be a pretty good chance that the rest of the engine may need a complete overhaul. Premature timing chain failure could be the result of poor engine maintenance, basically, from a lack of regular oil changes and other routine maintenance. The best thing you can do if you hear any abnormal noises in the current car you are driving, or the car you may consider buying, is to have a trusted mechanic take a listen to it for you, to be 100% sure. How do you tell if an engine has a timing chain? One way is to tell is that usually a timing chain can be enclosed underneath a metal or aluminum cover. It is lubricated by the engine's oil and needs to be in a sealed environment.

The most important things to look at under the hood of a car you are considering buying are the fluids—not just the level of the fluids, but the color of the fluids. The first fluid we are going to talk about is the engine oil. Most individuals know the importance of changing engine oil, but the question is: How often did they change it? The best example would be service records, but what if they are not available? How does engine oil get dirty? Engine oil is exposed to great temperatures, blow-by of unburned fuel, and carbon that gets past the piston rings. Over time, the motor oil thins out from fuel absorption. Its ability to lubricate and remove friction and heat is greatly diminished. When you pull the dipstick out to inspect the oil, wipe it off and reinsert the dipstick back in the tube. Pull the dipstick out, once again, to retrieve a true oil level reading. Most oil measuring dipsticks have two dots or lines. The top dot or line indicates that the oil level is good. The bottom line or dot indicates that the oil level is one quart low. If the engine oil is low, it could be for two basic reasons.

The first reason could be that the engine is leaking oil from somewhere. Secondly, the engine could be using oil—in other words, it is burning oil. Some engines will use oil, and some will not use as much. In most cases it can be considered normal for an engine to use a little oil. What is normal oil consumption for an engine? This can vary from manufacturer to manufacturer. Normal oil consumption can differ. This is why it is important for you to inspect your engine's oil level on a regular basis. Let's say you go 4,000 miles between oil changes. It's been 3,000 miles since you changed your oil; you check your oil level, and it's a quart low. Don't panic—this can be considered normal. Just add a quart of oil and change it when it's due for 4,000 miles. If it's been only 1,000 miles since you changed your oil last and your oil is a quart low, that could be a problem, especially if you see blue smoke in your rearview mirror. When you pull the engine oil dipstick out of the vehicle you are thinking of buying, and the oil looks black as coal, be suspicious. Be especially suspicious if the oil level is low. Take a look to see if there is an oil change reminder sticker in the upper left-hand side of the windshield, to determine when the oil was last changed.

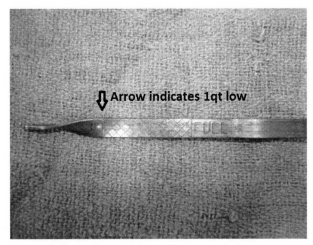

The most important and most forgotten item in your car—
the engine oil dipstick. Do not ignore it!

Automatic transmission fluid

This fluid should appear red in color in most vehicles. This fluid should not smell burnt. If you are not sure what burnt transmission fluid smells like, get a new container of automatic transmission fluid, open it up, and see what new automatic transmission fluid smells like. Burnt automatic transmission fluid has a very strong odor to it. When you pull the dipstick out of the transmission, take a close look at the color of the transmission fluid. If the fluid is close to black in color, with a strong odor to it, you may want to close the hood of the car and look at something different.

A vehicle that has transmission fluid that is black will more than likely have shifting issues or slippage due to the previous owner's lack of maintenance. Need I mention again—ask for service records! Imagine an automatic transmission as a big pump. It is actually a hydraulic pump that performs an enormous amount of work, day in and day out. If you do not take care of your automatic transmission by replacing the fluid at recommended intervals, your transmission will take care of your wallet, by making it considerably lighter! If you have the opportunity to talk to or contact the previous owner of the vehicle you are thinking of buying, ask them if they ever replaced the transmission fluid. If they did, ask them if they replaced the transmission filter if applicable when they had the transmission serviced.

Brake fluid

Brake fluid should appear almost clear or tan in color. It should never appear green or dark brown. If the vehicle you are thinking of purchasing is over three years old, chances are that brake fluid is over three years old too. Over time, brake fluid collects moisture. When brake fluid is new, it has a boiling point of around 450°F. Over time, brake fluid attracts moisture. The more moisture it attracts, the more it lowers the brake fluid's boiling point. If it is not replaced every two years or so, it will gradually hamper your braking performance, especially when your brakes get hot. Moisture-laden brake fluid can also wreak havoc on the internal components of a hydraulic braking system, as well as the internal components of your ABS system.

Clutch master cylinder fluid

The clutch master cylinder uses the same fluid your brake system uses. This fluid *is* brake fluid. If the vehicle has a manual transmission, you will find a small reservoir, with a removable cap, usually located next to the brake master cylinder. This fluid should appear light tan or almost clear in color. It should never be dark brown or green. If it is discolored, this indicates that the seals in the master cylinder and the slave cylinder are likely deteriorated. When this fluid is dark brown or black, it could quite possibly mean that the seals in the clutch master cylinder, or slave cylinder, are leaking or starting to leak. When the brake fluid is green, it can indicate the loss of copper lining inside the steel brake line.

Power steering fluid

Many automotive manufacturers use automatic transmission fluid for power steering fluid. If so, this fluid should appear red in color. Some manufacturers use a specialty fluid for their power steering systems. It can appear nearly clear or light brown in color. This fluid should never appear black! If the fluid is black, it could be a telltale sign of deterioration of the seals within the steering rack and pump assembly. Pay close attention to any noises, while steering the vehicle when it is running, but not moving. If you hear a moaning-type noise when turning the steering wheel from 11 o'clock to one o'clock, it may indicate an issue with the power steering pump.

Antifreeze

Automotive manufacturers use many different colors when it comes to the engine's antifreeze or coolant. It can be red, blue, orange, pink—or, most commonly, green. Warning! Make sure, if you remove the radiator cap, that the engine has not been running and it is cold. After removing the radiator cap, look into the radiator. Coolant should not look cloudy and should never have oil mixed in with the coolant. When oil gets into the engine's cooling system, it will have a milky appearance. It separates from the coolant, just like oil and water do.

Another good place to look is in the coolant reservoir located either on the right or the left side of the radiator; there should not be any oil or residue in the reservoir. Most coolant reservoirs have a minimum and maximum level. The level should be at the full mark. The reservoir should never be overfull. This may indicate an overheating issue, such as a blown head gasket or cracked cylinder head. That would be a worst-case scenario. Hopefully, an overfull reservoir may only be a bad radiator cap. If the reservoir is empty, this may indicate that the engine is burning up the antifreeze. This can be considered normal, in some cases, as some service stations do not top off fluids as they should, during routine maintenance. It is not abnormal for a vehicle to use small amounts of coolant, in most cases. If your coolant reservoir is not getting topped off, when you get your car serviced, an air pocket can form in your engine's cooling system. When this happens, it does not allow the coolant to flow as it should. Your engine can overheat as a result, causing engine damage. This is comparable to what would happen if you were to get an air bubble in your bloodstream—not good.

The battery

The top surface of the battery should appear clean. It should have no signs of corrosion on the battery positive or negative terminals. A lot of corrosion on the battery terminals indicates that the battery is leaking acid around the battery posts. This battery may test good. However, it would be strongly recommended that this battery be discarded. This could also indicate that the vehicle's charging system may be overcharging and boiling the acid from the battery. Ask the salesman or the person you are buying the vehicle from if it has the original battery, or if it has been replaced. If the vehicle has the original battery and let's say it's four years old, the salesman may say the battery tested okay. That is fine; however, a battery that is four years old may not last much longer. You must understand that anything can happen, especially in subzero temperatures and the extreme heat of summertime. A battery four to five years old that has been tested okay still could fail without any warning, winter or summer. Keep that in mind. Never create a spark around a battery, especially when it is charging. It can explode! It is also important for you to know that a vehicle's charging system cannot be tested with a bad battery. The battery must always be tested before the charging system.

Corroded battery terminal post.

Note this badly leaking battery terminal post. It can be cleaned with baking soda and water. This is only a temporary solution. The battery pictured is eight years old and needs to be replaced. The charging system needs to be checked for a possible overcharging condition that may be boiling the acid out of the battery. Caution: If you see a battery like this, avoid contact with it and the corrosion. It will burn you!

Fluid inspections in greater detail will appear in the chapter titled Fluid Maintenance. Any vehicles with four-wheel drive have final drive fluids that need to be inspected with the vehicle on a hoist. Hopefully in this chapter you have gained some insight into what to look for under the hood of a vehicle you are considering purchasing. Many of these under- the-hood items we have talked about this chapter are the obvious ones that you need to be concerned about. If you have any doubt about what you are looking at, make sure to have your mechanic give you a second opinion if needed. Don't forget to bring along your flashlight!

CHAPTER 5

How to Notice Collision Work

Can you see where this car was damaged?

O ne of the worst feelings you can have after purchasing a used car is having a friend, who may know a little bit more about cars than you do, telling you they notice some bad paint-work or bodywork the car has had done in the past. How about when you bring your "new" used car in for its first service, only to have the mechanic tell you the car has significant rust issues?

This is a hard pill to swallow, especially when you have just purchased the car.

In the previous chapter, discussing knowing what to look and listen for under the hood, I briefly discussed missing vehicle identification tags. These tags or labels will indicate whether a hood, trunk lid, or door has been replaced. All of these tags should match the vehicle identification tag located at the left lower corner of the dashboard. Most auto body repair shops do not take the time to remove these labels and reapply them to the new body component that has just been replaced. The extra time needed to swap the labels or tags may not be included in the original body repair estimate. Most body repair shops have gone to the flat-rate pay system. If the body repair man gets 2 hours to replace, prime, and paint a fender or hood, that is all he is likely to do. When you open a door, the engine compartment hood or trunk lid, make sure you look for these tags. If any of these tags are missing, this would indicate that bodywork has been performed on the vehicle in the past. Please remember that not all manufacturers use these vehicle identification tags. You may have to look closely for other clues, such as overspray, poor paint work, and uneven or poorly aligned body panels.

If you need significant body work done because you got in a little fender bender, I suggest that you find a body shop that is not flat rate—that is, if you can find one. Another obstacle is finding an insurance company that deals with a non-flat-rate pay system. You should experience good quality work performed on your car. You should also know that to keep costs low, insurance companies may attempt to replace damaged body components with used body components on your car. *Yes—used parts.*

Take a walk around the vehicle and check for poor bodywork. The first thing I want you to do is walk to the front right corner of the vehicle. Kneel down and look down the entire side of the vehicle. What you need to look for is any deviation from a straight line, such as waves in the body panel or uneven surfaces, such as leading edges of doors sticking out farther than the trailing body panels. Also look for paint overspray. What is overspray, you may ask? The best example I can give you is to look closely in the fender wells of the vehicle. Let's say the vehicle is white. You would look closely at fender wells for white powdery overspray on what is supposed to be a black wheel well. You may also see it almost anywhere on the vehicle—look for overspray on anything that may be chrome, or trim; usually if the body repair man gets lazy, he may just try to tape off the trim instead of removing it before painting. I'm not saying it is bad to tape over chrome or trim before painting; however, if it does happen and overspray is on the chrome, it should be cleaned off before being delivered to the customer.

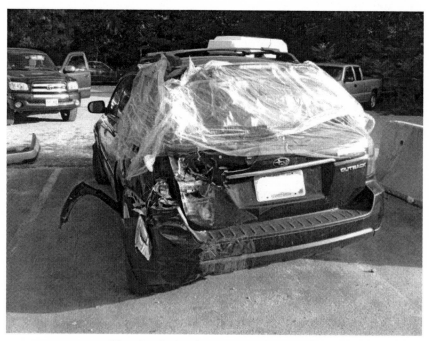

That is where the car was damaged.

Body filler

I will share with you a little trick I learned a long time ago. Before you leave home to go look at a used car, you may want to bring along little flexible refrigerator magnet to take with you. These magnets work best because they will not scratch the paint, if you are careful. If you notice any questionable bodywork on a vehicle, you can try to stick the magnet to that spot. If the magnet does not stick to that spot, this would tell you that the vehicle has had body filler used in it. If the magnet does not stick to the metal portion of the vehicle's body, move the magnet to a nearby spot and see if it sticks to that. If it does, this may tell you that the body has had plastic body filler used in it.

One thing you need to realize, however—there are not a lot of vehicles out there that do not have plastic body filler in them. Even the factories that manufacture the vehicle have been known to use plastic filler, to smooth out imperfections before the vehicle is painted. Please keep in mind that some automotive manufacturers use plastic fenders and doors. Saturn is famous for this. Nearly all passenger cars today have plastic bumpers. You will obviously not get a magnet to stick there. Painted plastic bumpers should not have any cracks in the paint. If you do notice cracks in the paint on any plastic body component, this would indicate that the body component may have been replaced and was not prepared properly before painting.

Another way to tell whether plastic filler has been used on the vehicle is if you notice bubbling under the paint. This could mean plastic filler may have been used to cover up rust. Since the rust was not completely removed, it can still form underneath the paint to cause a bubbling effect.

A little plastic filler is okay, but you want to stay away from a vehicle that has a lot of plastic filler in it. Please note this: almost all body shops will not guarantee rust work, period.

Check this out on left! The rust was painted over with a brush!
Nice job, Picasso!
Look at the white overspray on the black rocker panel on the right.

Peeling paint

Maybe you have seen it—a car coming at you that looks like it has been going so fast that the paint has peeled off the hood, the roof, or the trunk of the car. GM and Chrysler seem to have had a problem with this in the '80s and '90s. Not many people realized at the time that they could get their car repainted under warranty. Bodywork is not my profession or specialty, but I have been told about it by several people in the auto body repair business who witnessed this phenomenon firsthand. The factory did not apply enough primer to the metal surfaces of the vehicles that were to be painted. I have also been told that other steps in the painting process had been improperly performed, causing the paint to peel off the cars. A good body shop or body repair man will take the time needed to prepare a vehicle properly before painting.

Photo on left shows what can happen when you don't touch up that little paint chip.
Photo on right shows what happens when rust returns under plastic filler.

Rust

Rust is rust and it is fairly easy to notice on the exterior of the vehicle; in most cases, rust is easier to spot than bad collision work. Anywhere there is winter, there will be more rusty vehicles than any other place in the country, mostly because of the amount of salt that is used on our roads and highways. The fact that most people don't take the time—or have the time, for that matter—to wash their vehicle causes the road salt to slowly eat away at their car. Maybe you live close to the ocean and frequently visit the beach. This can also slowly eat away at your car.

There are many things that a person can do to keep salt and rust from eating away at their cars. Most important is washing the car thoroughly, especially under the vehicle and in the wheel wells. Most drive-through car washes will spray the undercarriage with a high-pressure rinse, to wash away all that nasty salt from the underside of your investment. Once the rust starts on a vehicle, there is really no stopping it. A car can be well undercoated with hydraulic oil that is compatible with any rubber components under the vehicle. For example, if someone is to use used engine oil to try to stop the growth of rust under the vehicle, it may stop the rust; however, any rubber component that used engine oil comes in contact with will be destroyed, as the oil will soften the rubber. You should use only hydraulic oil or used or new automatic transmission fluid to try to deter the cancerous rust from destroying your vehicle. *You should find an environmentally responsible shop that will oil undercoat your vehicle properly.*

We will talk more about rust in Chapter 7.

Mismatched paint

If you are colorblind, you may need some help with this one. In most cases, a really bad paint job is not hard to spot. However, even if the proper color code is used to match the paint, sometimes it won't; if the vehicle is older and the paint is faded, it won't match if the body shop has not taken the time to properly blend the new paint into the old paint. The best way to spot this is to bring the vehicle into a shop and put the car under fluorescent lights. Yes, believe it or not, you can spot more defects in the vehicle's paint job under fluorescent lights than under bright sunlight.

Black can be one of the hardest colors to notice if bodywork has been done or if the vehicle has been painted. Black paint is more susceptible to scratches—at least they show up a lot more. If you notice a body panel on a black car that is a lot more shiny and scratch-free than any of the other panels, this could mean that the body panel may have been refinished recently.

While we are talking about black cars—if you are thinking about buying a black vehicle, ask somebody who owns one. They will probably tell you that they will never own another black car as long as they live! Usually, the people who like their black cars have the extra money to pay someone to keep it buffed out and detailed on a regular basis. If you do buy a black car, get ready to use a lot of elbow grease on it to keep it looking nice! If you live in New England in the winter, it's not hard to spot a black car with salt all over it.

Orange peel

Another sign of poor paint work is what is called orange peel. The paint will have an orange peel-type texture to it. This is very obvious, because its texture does not match the smooth texture of the rest of the vehicle's paint. This will tell you that the vehicle has had paint work. The usual cause is that the painter laid the paint on a little too thick, resulting in an orange peel surface to the paint.

Remember, if you are not sure if the vehicle has had bodywork, make sure to ask for a CARFAX! Or bring the vehicle you are seriously interested in buying to a reputable auto body repair shop and ask them if they would mind checking the vehicle, to see if it has had any bodywork done. It is unbelievable what the trained eye can see that your untrained eye cannot. You also need to realize that most vehicles on the road today have had some type of bodywork done in their lifetime. Most of it is nothing to worry about. What you do need to be concerned about is a vehicle that may have been in a major collision and had significant damage. A vehicle like that will most certainly give you trouble in the future, such as uneven-wearing tires if not aligned properly, rattles, creaks ... oh yeah, and let's not forget electrical problems!

Oh—by the way, if you see a car with a salvage tag on the "A" pillar, walk away!

CHAPTER 6
Road Testing

This could quite possibly be the most important step when purchasing a new or used vehicle. More importantly, with a used car than a new car, you have to know what to look, listen, and feel for when going for a road test.

With a new car, you basically want to do all your homework. Preferably you are not looking at a new model year, so you can get the skinny, after several years of production, on how reliable the

vehicle may be. In other words, if you make the decision to purchase a new car, be sure that it is the next-to-last or the last year of
production, so almost all of the bugs are worked out of the vehicle.
You will not find any real, valid reliability reports for a new model
year vehicle. You are basically the guinea pig, if you decide to buy a
brand-new model year car.

If you get excited because you purchased a brand-new car that
was the tenth car produced for the new model year, you may want
to think about that. You would probably be better off purchasing
the 5,000th car produced for that model year. One other thing you
want to think about when buying a new or used car: Is it going to
be a comfortable car if you go on a long trip? Make sure you take
the car for a good long road test, to help you better determine if
the car will fit you comfortably. Better yet, ask someone who drives
a car like the one you want to purchase. There is no worse feeling
than arriving at your destination after a three-hour drive with a sore
back and numb legs! Of course some people like a firm mattress
and some prefer a soft mattress so be careful who you ask!

Before you leave home to go and road test some cars, it may
be helpful to you to equip yourself to take notes. If possible, you
should arrange for your mechanic to go for a ride with you, to assist
you in locating issues with the car that you are considering purchasing. This is a great thing to do, because if you notice some problems
or noises with the vehicle, you can pull over and write them down
as they may arise. Before you road test the vehicle, it is a good idea
to look underneath the vehicle to see if there are any signs of fluid
loss. If you do notice any oil, antifreeze, or transmission fluid on the
ground, you'll want to make sure whether the fluid loss has come
from the vehicle that is parked over the stain. Just remember, in
the summer months when the air conditioner is running in a car,
it is normal for water to drip out of the evaporator drain onto the
ground. Automobiles usually get moved around a lot at new car

dealerships and used car lots. That fluid on the pavement may have come from another vehicle that was parked in that spot previously. I will cover identifying fluid loss in Chapter 7.

When you get in the car before you road test, make sure you roll the driver's side window down. This will help you hear any strange noises the car may make when it is first started. Usually, when an engine is cold, it will make the most noise when first started. Make sure the radio is off! What I want you to listen for are knocking noises, belt squeals, and rattles. If you hear something, write it down. Perhaps later on, your mechanic can explain what the noise may be.

Before you start the car, I want you to look in the rearview mirror to check the tailpipe for abnormal exhaust. It is best if you can have someone else start the car for you, so you can see what first comes out of the tailpipe. Pay close attention to what comes out of the exhaust, when you first start the car. You will want to rev the car's engine up a little bit to see if you can produce any blue smoke from the tailpipe. If you do see blue smoke coming from the exhaust system, it indicates that the engine is using excessive amounts of oil. This is most likely a sign of a tired engine, which may have been poorly maintained in the past. It is not uncommon for an engine with higher mileage to use a little motor oil. After the engine is fully warmed and you are road testing it, accelerate the engine, and if blue smoke is coming from the tailpipe as you look in the rearview mirror, this is definitely a sign of a tired engine! If you see white smoke coming from the tailpipe, this could be considered normal—it may be only condensation that has built up, as a vehicle may have been sitting for some time.

After the engine is fully warmed, after a minute or so of driving the hot exhaust system should burn off any condensation that has been built up in the exhaust system. However, it may take a lot longer for this condensation to burn off in colder weather. After the vehicle has been fully warmed, if you notice white smoke coming from the exhaust system, this could be a sign of a problem with the engine's internal cooling system, such as a blown head gasket—or worse, a cracked cylinder head. It could quite possibly be very costly to fix. In this case, you may want to stay away from this vehicle! If you do notice that the white smoke does not go away after the engine is fully warmed, try to notice if the exhaust smells sweet. This will definitely indicate that the engine is using or burning anti-freeze. Keep in mind, however, that you will almost always have some white exhaust coming from the tailpipe in cold weather.

Once you finally get the car on the road, preferably a highway with a minimally crowned surface, I want you to check to see if the car pulls to one side of the road or the other. Make sure that the steering wheel is centered. If the steering wheel is not centered, it would indicate the vehicle may be out of alignment. It can be considered perfectly normal for a vehicle to pull to the right on a crowned road surface. On a nice flat stretch of highway that doesn't have a lot of bumps in the road—and make sure it is not a windy day—you should be able to gently rest your hands on the steering wheel briefly. Count one to five and a vehicle may start to drift to the right, which should be considered normal. A vehicle significantly out of alignment would be indicated by the amount that you have to struggle with the steering wheel to correct it to move straight forward.

If a vehicle pulls that much, it would indicate that the vehicle is significantly out of alignment, has a worn suspension component, or simply has a tire that is very low on air or nearly flat! A tire could also have a broken belt inside. Hopefully, before you road test the vehicle, you would notice a soft tire as you walk around to examine the outside of the vehicle. A good car salesman would not let you get into a car to road test it, with low tire pressures. However, you must understand that sometimes the car salesman is at the mercy of his mechanic. He or she may assume that the tire pressures are correct.

Brakes and Shakes

Check for vibrations at highway speeds. Most vibration issues at highway speeds can be corrected with a simple wheel balancing. A bent rim or unevenly worn tire can make it impossible to smooth the car out with balancing the rim; tires must be replaced in some cases. Pay close attention to vibrations when applying the brakes. If you feel a slight amount of vibration when braking and shrug it off and say that it's not so bad, you need to understand that in time it will only get worse. It may need the brake rotors and drums machined or replaced in the near future. What causes this condition? Over time, the brake rotors and drums are exposed to great changes in temperature. They get hot, they cool down, they get hot—and you drive through a puddle of water and they cool down very quickly! This can cause the brake rotors to warp when you depress the brake pedal. This warped condition, or run out, transmits through your brakes. You will feel the vibration in the steering wheel, or a pulsation via the brake pedal. Also, if at some point the wheels on the vehicle were over-tightened, it could cause the brake rotors to warp.

Before you start a vehicle, if you press on the brake pedal and start the engine, the brake pedal should sink slightly. This will indicate to you that the brakes' power boosting system is working properly. If the brake pedal feels hard as a rock, there could be a problem with the brake booster system. If the brake pedal feels soft or spongy, this could be an indication of many things. Firstly, air in the brake lines could be a cause of this. A repair could have been done to the brake system's hydraulic components, and it is possible that the system was not bled properly to remove all air in the system. Secondly—and more commonly—brake pads can get stuck in the caliper brackets, or there is a stuck or frozen caliper slide or piston. Lastly and most alarmingly, the brake system's master cylinder could be faulty. Your brake pedal may feel very spongy and slowly go to the floor. If this is the case, you may suspect that the brake system's master cylinder is faulty.

Axles

Next, you should drive the vehicle to a big paved parking lot that is fairly empty. Come to a complete stop and turn the steering wheel all the way to the right until the steering wheel stops. Now accelerate the vehicle and drive it in a complete circle and come to a stop. Now do the same thing, but steer the car to the left in a complete circle and come to a stop. When doing this, if you notice a loud clicking noise from the front end, it indicates that the vehicle has bad axles or bad constant velocity joints. All vehicles today with front-wheel drive have constant velocity joints, usually called CV joints for short. If the vehicle has four-wheel drive and you hear a growling noise coming from the rear end while making the sharp turns, it is likely that there could be a problem with the vehicle's rear differential.

Manual Transmission

When you're driving a car that has a manual transmission, you want to make sure upon taking off that the clutch pedal does not release too high. You want to have the clutch pedal release just before halfway—if not, this could be a sign of excessive clutch disc wear. When shifting the transmission into gear and then releasing it, the car should not shake or vibrate. You should experience only a smooth engagement. Before you hit the road with the car, push the clutch all the way to the floor and shift through all the gears. It should shift into all the gears smoothly; if not, this could mean weak springs in the clutch disc. You should not have to double clutch to get the car to go into gear. In some vehicles it may be necessary to double clutch to get the transmission into reverse. This can be considered normal in some vehicles. Make sure that the vehicle's floor mat is not wedged under the clutch pedal, restricting the pedal. If the car shifts okay when the engine is not running, this definitely means the clutch needs to be replaced! When the springs in the clutch disc get really weak, it is sometimes impossible to shift the transmission into gear. If the clutch assembly is not replaced soon, it could cause permanent damage to the transmission by trying to force it into gear.

When you are on the road with the car, try shifting the vehicle into fourth or fifth gear at a low speed; then slowly push the accelerator to the floor. If the car has an RPM gauge—or in other words, a tachometer—watch it as you do this. If the engine revs up as the speed of the vehicle does not increase, this means the clutch is more than likely worn out. As we say in the business, the clutch is toasted! If the vehicle lugs or chugs, the vehicle has a good clutch. This tells you that there is no slippage between the clutch disc and flywheel. As far as knowing the last time the oil was changed in the manual transmission, it is important to have service records available for the used car you are thinking of purchasing. If you buy the car and you have no idea when the manual transmission oil has been changed, you should just go ahead and have it changed to remove all doubt. In most cases, changing the manual gear box oil requires minimal labor; it is fairly inexpensive to replace it. Make sure that you use the correct fluid recommended by the manufacturer.

Wheel Bearings

In my career, I have seen many customers who have purchased new tires because they thought their old tires were noisy on the road. The fact is that their car had a bad wheel bearing. A noisy wheel bearing can be tricky to diagnose. I will explain to you as best I can what a bad one sounds like. You will usually hear a droning, humming, vibrating sound at various speeds. The noise will change in pitch and in tone as you load and unload the weight on the suspected wheel bearing.

When there are no other cars on the road, to test your car, slowly swerve the car right to left. When you do this, the suspected bad wheel bearing will get louder and quieter as you load and unload the wheel that has the bad bearing.

How do you tell the difference between a noisy wheel bearing and a noisy tire? Usually, if you have a genuinely noisy tire, it is because the surface of the tire is choppy and worn unevenly. You can usually see it or feel it, by moving your hand over the surface of the tire. Be careful of steel cords sticking out of the tire! Road noise from a choppy tire will not usually change as you swerve the car slowly from left to right. If the car you were driving had a suspected bad wheel bearing on the right front, but the tire was in question, here's what you can do. Take the wheel and tire from the right front and move it to the right rear. If the noise moves to the right rear, you know that you have a noisy tire. If the noise stays in the right front, you have yourself a bad wheel bearing.

Automatic Transmission

Unlike a manual transmission, most automatic transmissions have a dipstick to check the level and condition of the fluid. I strongly suggest that you check to see what the fluid looks like, as I mentioned in the previous chapter. Just as important is what the fluid smells like. First off, if the vehicle has an owner's manual in the glove box, they can direct you to the location of the transmission dipstick.

Please note that some manufacturers do not use a dipstick to check transmission fluid level and may require vehicle to be on a hoist to inspect the fluid.

Once you find the dipstick and pull it out, the fluid should look red or pinkish in color. It should not look brown, and it definitely should not look black. If the fluid looks black and has a burnt smell to it, close the hood and find another car to look at! That black stuff is more than likely clutch material that is no longer adhering to clutch disk where it should be.

We will talk much more about fluids and the importance of replacing them in the maintenance section of this book.

Let's move on to road testing a car with an automatic transmission. I want you to start the car and apply the brake. Shift from park to drive, then neutral to reverse and park position. You should not hear any loud clunks, bangs, or ratcheting noises. Also there should not be any whining or growling noises when shifting gears. There should not be a long delay between shifting from neutral to drive or reverse before the transmission engages; this could indicate excessive differential wear. Pay close attention to the way the vehicle takes off. Make sure that it does not bog down. For example, make sure it does not start moving in high gear, such as fourth or overdrive. This would be very obvious if it were to happen.

When pulling the car onto the highway, accelerate to highway speed with light to moderate acceleration. The transmission should shift smoothly and evenly, with no banging into gears. The transmission should not slip into gear either. By this, I mean that the transmission should not gradually roll into gear; this should be a positive shift. In other words, there should be no long delay between shifts. For example, there should be a positive shift between first to second gear, second to third gear, third gear to fourth gear, and overdrive. If there is slippage between gears, this could be an early indication that the vehicle will eventually not move, and that is when things get really pricey!

An automatic transmission that bangs into gear may not be as serious as it sounds. It may be only a shift solenoid issue or shift cable that is out of adjustment. The trick is to get to the root of the problem before that harsh shift causes internal transmission damage. I don't mean to sound redundant, but an automatic transmission can be one of the most unpredictable and most expensive items repaired on nearly any vehicle. If you have doubts about the way the transmission shifts, you could ask the salesperson or person that you are thinking of buying a car from if your mechanic could take a listen to it. Or just move on to a different vehicle with the same type transmission and see if it shifts the same by comparison to know for sure.

Don't worry about being a pain to the salesperson; it's your wallet on the line here. If the transmission fails, you just might have to pay for it! One very important thing that I almost forgot to mention: Does the vehicle have a trailer hitch or signs of having had a trailer hitch? Did the previous owner follow the guidelines in the owner's manual for towing with this vehicle? If the vehicle has a tow hitch on it, these valuable questions to follow should be answered. What did they tow with the vehicle? What was the maximum towing capacity of the vehicle?

If you are thinking of buying a truck that has had a snow plow on it, more than likely this truck has seen some work. Well, that's what trucks are for—work; however, you can still take care of them. To my customers who use a truck with automatic transmission for plowing, I strongly recommend exchanging the transmission fluid every season. I can personally say that most of the trucks out there with plows on them need to get that type of loving care from people who own them. I'm not saying these people are careless people, but they are not informed about changing their transmission fluid more often when plowing. Quite frankly, it will not matter if the transmission fluid is changed every year, if they do not plow with the truck in low range. Plowing snow in high range will quickly shorten the life of an automatic transmission.

Power Steering

It is fairly easy to identify any problems with power steering. It is obvious if there is a problem with the power steering system, because the car won't steer easily. More than likely, the power steering pump will be excessively noisy. When you get in the car and start it up, turn the wheel all the way to the right and all the way to the left; there should not be any belt squeals or any difficulty in the range of movement when steering. Low tire pressure can make a vehicle steer hard, too. This may mislead you to believe that there is a problem with the power steering system. If the vehicle you are road testing steers hard, you may want to check the fluid level to see if it is low. Most power steering fluid reservoirs have a minimum and maximum fluid level. If the fluid level is at or below minimum, this may indicate that there is a leak in the power steering hydraulic system, causing the fluid to be at the minimum level. If the power steering fluid level is fine, and the power steering seems to come and go, this could mean that the vehicle may have a seized steering shaft U joint. In this case, the U joint would need to be replaced to correct the issue.

Basically, when you road test any vehicle it is important that you drive the vehicle on both smooth and bumpy roads to expose it to every possible road condition that could make any hidden rattles or other noises appear. You should make every effort to drive the vehicle as much as possible before you buy it. You do not want these noises to appear after you have purchased a vehicle! Try to road test a car when the roads are dry. Usually, wet road conditions will cover up noises you would normally hear when the roads are dry.

After you are done road testing, stop and let the vehicle idle. Pay close attention to the engine's temperature gauge. It should stay just below halfway. Continue to let the vehicle idle and wait for the engine's cooling fan to cycle. You should be able to hear the fan run. If you are unsure if the fan has run or not, pop the hood. Continue to let the engine idle and wait for the fan to run. If the fan does not run, take another look at the engine's temperature gauge and make sure that it is not climbing toward hot. If the fan does not run, there's a problem with the engine's cooling system that needs to be looked at before you purchase the vehicle. After you shut the vehicle off, take another look underneath the vehicle to make sure that it is not losing any fluid. I know I told you to do this in the beginning before you road test the vehicle; however, it is important to do this again after the road test, after the engine has been fully warmed up.

Checking the Interior of the Vehicle

This is one of the items most often overlooked when buying a used car. What I mean by checking the interior of the car is checking everything! Simply put: If you see a switch or button, make sure that it actually operates whatever it is supposed to operate.

Check each door to see if it opens from the inside and out. Most state safety inspections require the windows and doors to function to pass inspection. Make sure that if the vehicle is equipped with power windows, every window in the vehicle functions up and down. With vehicles that do not have power windows, make sure the windows crank up and crank down with minimal effort. Needless to say, it is important that the window crank does not come off in your hand!

Look inside the trunk and make sure that the car is equipped with a spare tire, jack, and all of the necessary tools that you will need to change a flat tire. Believe me, it is no fun to find out that you do not have a spare tire when you have a flat tire on vacation! If the vehicle is equipped with wheel locks, make sure the wheel lock key is in the vehicle! I have seen vehicles towed in to the dealership with a flat tire because the individual who owned the car did not know that the car had wheel locks! In this case, the wheel lock key was in the glove box all along. A wheel lock is a specially designed lug nut, usually only one per wheel that can be removed only with a special socket/key. Make sure that the spare tire is properly inflated. In most cases, spare tire pressures NEVER get checked. Many vehicles are equipped with a space-saver spare tire. Most of them require 60 PSI to inflate them properly. I'll give you a little tip—when you take your car in for service and you ask to have your spare tire pressure checked, make sure you do not have a trunk full of stuff! This will make for an unhappy mechanic working on your car, and you don't want that. When you look in the trunk's spare tire well, make sure the bottom of it is not full of water or showing signs of water staining. There is nothing worse than finding out that your new used car has a water leak in the trunk. It gets moldy and stinky!

Checking the Heater and Air Conditioning Systems

Checking the heater, especially in New England, is a very important step. When buying a car in the summer months, who wants to see if the heater works, when it's 85 to 90 degrees outside! On the other side of the coin, who checks to see if the air conditioner is working in the middle of the winter when it's 20 to 30 degrees outside? Make sure the temperature control works freely and easily with no binding. Be sure that all the positions are functional, especially the defrost mode. We touched on road testing the vehicle and keeping an eye on the engine's temperature gauge. In the winter, if you notice that the temperature gauge is struggling to climb to just before halfway, where it needs to be, and the heat that the car is delivering from the vents seems warm but not hot, it could mean that the vehicle needs a thermostat replaced.

You should also check to make sure that no antifreeze is leaking into the interior of the vehicle from the heater core. The heater core is a small radiator-like component that is installed under the center lower portion of the dashboard. The heater core itself is not a very expensive component; however, it is usually expensive to replace, because there is so much labor involved to replace the component. This is simply because the whole dashboard needs to be removed to expose a faulty heater core. Another warning sign of a leaking heater core would be fogging of the windows in defrost mode. Also, a sweet smell of antifreeze would be coming through the vents. Please keep your pets away from any coolant leaks, as it will in most cases be fatal to them if they ingest it.

Check to make sure that all fan speeds are available. Most vehicles usually have four fan speeds. If you notice that some of the fan speeds are missing, this is usually an indication that the fan system has a bad blower resistor. A blower fan resistor is fairly inexpensive to replace in most cases—that is, if it is not a specialty car. If you notice that when the fan speed is on high, the volume of air coming out of vents seems low, this could mean that the car may have a plugged cabin air filter. Many vehicles today are equipped with a cabin air filter or pollen filter, and many people do not know that the car has one. These filters are supposed to be replaced every 15,000 miles or so depending on how dusty the conditions are.

There are many cars out on the road with 60,000 to 90,000 miles on them with an original cabin filter! At this point in time, the filters get so plugged with debris that they cannot allow air to pass through as they were designed to do. Basically it's like placing a towel on the back side of the fan—not much air comes out the front, does it? Cabin air filters are relatively inexpensive, and in most cases are easy to replace. It is important to know also that the vehicle was not ever in a flood. It can be a little bit scary, not knowing what the vehicle may have been flooded with, and not knowing what kind of bacteria could be growing inside the vent system. This is why it is important to check CARFAX.com.

Audio System/ DVD System

With all we have covered so far, you want to make sure that the car or van you buy has a functioning audio system. In the beginning of this chapter I suggested that you come equipped to take notes while you are on the road test. You should also grab a CD or DVD to make sure that they are functional. It is very disappointing to find out that the previous owner's children used the CD/ DVD player as a piggy bank! I have seen it many times.

If the sound system has an anti-theft system, make sure that the special code is available with the car. You will need this code to make your radio work again, if your battery goes completely dead. The five- or six-digit code should be available on a card, about the size of a credit card, in the glove box or with the owner's manual. If you are fortunate enough to be buying the vehicle from the original owner, they should have all of that for you. If the vehicle came from auction, the glove box will more than likely be empty in most cases. Make sure all speakers function, and that the fader and balancer functions work.

After-market Accessories

What is an after-market accessory? This is a component added to the vehicle that is not manufactured by the company that made the car. If you purchased a used vehicle with an after-market component and there is something wrong with it, you may be on your own. Chances are you won't be able to find out who installed the component or accessory. It may not be available to replace if you need a new one.

Aftermarket Remote Car Starters

Here is something that can be easily overlooked: an after-market remote car starter/security system. Yes, it's the convenience of not having to go out in the cold to start your car; instead, you can simply push a button from inside your house or from work. It results in a nice warm car in the winter or a nice cool car in summer. Sometimes there is more to it than that. If you notice a remote on the key ring and it is not marked with the car manufacturer's name, , chances are it is not a factory-installed remote car start system. I can easily spot an after-market remote start security system. It may not be that easy for you, but I will help you so you can spot one, and not by just looking at the remote control as I previously mentioned. Look in the owner's manual it usually has a layout of the gauges and warning lamps. If there are any extra LED lamps installed in a strange place that not coincide with the dashboard warning lamp layout in the owner's manual, chances are it is not factory-installed. Take a peek under the dash and see if there are any wires hanging down. See if there are any scotch locks connecting the wires together. These can be a dead giveaway that it is not a factory system. What is a scotch lock? A scotch lock is usually blue in color and is about the same diameter as a dime, and about a quarter-inch thick. Through the years I have removed many after-market remote start security systems. Seeing the electrical nightmares they have caused in the past does not make me want to go out and install one in my vehicle anytime soon! Let me tell you why. Imagine your alarm system going off at 2:30 a.m. for no apparent reason, and waking up your neighborhood. Nobody will like you, for sure. Or just imagine trying to start your car and the battery has gone dead. All of a sudden the system's control unit wakes up every relay in the system and decides it is going to drain your battery completely, not to mention starting your day off on the wrong foot. Or how about getting out of your car with it still running, to get the mail; you close the door behind you, and all the doors lock! Yes, all by themselves. With your child inside!

I also heard another scary story from a local shop. A gentleman just had his car repaired and went in to pay his bill. The man asked where his car was parked. The service advisor pointed out the window and said, "It's right outside." He pointed out the window into the parking lot. It was a cold winter day, so just after the service advisor handed him his keys, the car owner pushed the button on his remote to start his car. Not only did his car start outside in the lot, but there was another car in the shop that had the identical type of system, and it started too! It started while the mechanic was working on the car! Luckily for the mechanic, he was not working under the car. He was only doing a brake job. Just imagine what would've happened if the mechanic had been under the hood replacing belts! It just so happened these two remote car starters shared the same frequency. Keep in mind that remote car starters have come a long way since this happened with an old-style remote car starter system. The chances of this happening today, with a newer-style remote car starter system, would be extremely rare.

If you are buying a used car and it has remnants of an after-market security system, take my advice, and have it removed. Doing so will be sure to save you some headaches down the road. Most of today's automobiles have control systems that are very sensitive. Some do not like the electrical company that they are keeping, so to speak, with after-market add-ons. You may be asking for trouble if you have one of these electrical parasites installed in your car. If you absolutely must have one of these systems installed, have it done by someone who has been doing it for a while. Get the names of at least three customers who have had systems installed in their cars. Don't be afraid to call them and ask if they are happy with their systems.

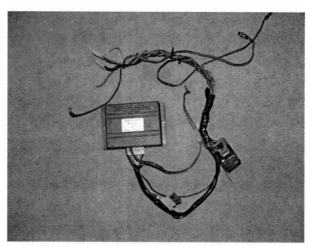

After-market security system removed from car.
This system was causing the customer's battery to
go dead time after time. How about that—it worked!
No one can steal a car when the battery is dead!

Non-factory-installed Sunroofs

Firstly, if a car or truck has had a sunroof installed and you think that it increases the value of the car or truck, think again. You must remember the vehicle has been cut into. There are two types of sunroofs. The first is the non-powered type, manual open and manual close sunroof. You don't usually have too many problems with this type, just as long as it doesn't leak! The second type would be the power sunroof. One of the biggest problems with this type of roof is the drain on each corner of the sunroof. These drains are basically four tubes connected to a pan-type tray. Hopefully the installer took the time to properly route the drain tubes, so the water does not leak into the vehicle. I have seen some poor installations over the years where the drain tubes leaked over the inside of the fuse box, causing many electrical issues ... many expensive electrical issues!

I can remember a story, years ago, where a woman had just gotten back from vacation and had her car parked at the airport for a week. When she was away on vacation, there had been quite a snowstorm in the area. She had approximately a foot of snow on top of her car. In a hurry, she did not clean the snow off the roof. She cleaned off only the windows and the hood of the car. So she drove off. She got on the highway and all of a sudden her sunroof decided to open, while she was driving down the highway! Guess where that foot of snow went? Yes, that's right—on her head and lap! And yes, it was an after-market installed power sunroof. Buyers beware!

CHAPTER 7
Looking Under the Car

In this chapter I want you to be able identify fluid leaks, structural rust issues, and missing or loose components. After all the years that I have been an automotive technician, one of the most satisfying things for me is to bring a customer out into the shop, so they can actually take a look at the underside of their car on a lift. It is so much easier for me, as a mechanic, to explain to the customer what exactly is going on with their car. Most importantly, I will more than likely earn their trust. Most people will never see or have the opportunity to look at the underside of the vehicle. Even if they do, they may not know exactly what they are looking at. Over the years I have seen a handful of times where somebody has purchased a used car and they are boasting about what a great deal they got and how perfect it is, only to be disappointed when they got their first oil change done. Or they are surprised at their first state inspection when they find out the vehicle is badly rusted and is not structurally sound. This can be a real let-down, especially if you bought the car as-is.

If you are thinking of purchasing a vehicle from a dealership or a used car lot, it may be fairly easy to ask your salesman if you can have your potential vehicle put on a lift, so you can take a look underneath the car. It is possible that you may be told that customers cannot be out in the shop, because their insurance won't cover you if you get hurt in the shop. This should not be a problem if someone from the dealership or repair shop accompanies you as they put the vehicle up on a lift. It especially should not be a problem if they want to sell you a car.

Let's say that you've done the road test in the vehicle. You pretty much like the car, but you would like to take a look at the underside. If you think of it before you leave home to go car shopping, it may be a good idea to have a flashlight handy so you can better see what you are looking at under the car. However, any well-equipped shop should have light you can use. *Also you need to remember that as you will be looking up at the vehicle, you should wear eye protection as debris could possibly fall into your eyes. It is better to be safe than sorry!* So please, wear <u>eye protection</u>!

Now that you have the car in the air, let's start at the right front wheel. If the vehicle is a front-wheel drive car I want you to take a close look at the <u>axles</u>. From the transmission to the wheel, you should see a shaft that connects to the wheel from the transmission. Each axle has an inner axle joint and outer axle joint. These axle joints have an accordion-shaped rubber boot for each joint. If you can, have somebody turn the steering wheel all the way to the right or left for you take a close look at the axle boot and make sure there are no signs of cracks in the boots.

Note dry rot cracking in axle boot. This boot can be replaced, saving the axle from being permanently damaged, and saving you money!

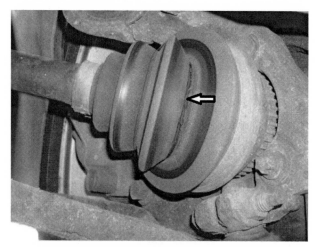

Arrow indicates dry crack in axle boot.
This axle can be saved by replacing the boot now.

If you do see cracks in the boots, this isn't always bad, because you can replace the axle boots before they rip open and lose all of the axle grease. It is far less expensive to replace a simple rubber boot than it is to replace the whole axle. If you do see a boot that is ripped open and has lost all the grease, it is best to replace that axle. I want you to go to the left front wheel and turn the wheel all the way to the left and examine that outer boot for cracks, as well. Keep in mind that if the vehicle is an all-wheel drive car you will have axle boots in the rear, as well. However, these axle boots are less prone to cracks, because the rear wheels do not turn to the left or right—unless the vehicle has rear-wheel steering, which is rare.

Too late! This axle needs to be replaced.
Note axle grease lost and that the axle joint is ruined.

I would like you to look at the <u>exhaust system.</u> Let's say you don't know what the exhaust system looks like, so start at the tailpipe at the rear of the car and work your way forward. Please be careful not to touch any of the components in the exhaust system, as you have just taken the car off the road from the road test. All components of the exhaust system will be hot! What you need to look for in the exhaust system is any signs of black carbon, anywhere in the system, caused by a leak. External rust on any exhaust system can be considered normal. When the exhaust system is new, it does not look new for long. What usually happens is that the exhaust system is also affected by condensation buildup within the system when it cools down. This condensation within the system can cause exhaust and rust from the inside out, ultimately causing a leak. On some exhaust systems you may notice a small hole on the bottom of the muffler. This is part of the muffler design. It allows condensation to drain through this hole, in an effort to minimize condensation in the muffler. If you see black carbon stains outside and around this drain hole, this can be considered normal. However, I am not a fan of these systems that have a condensation drain hole. Most vehicles today come with stainless steel exhaust systems. These systems usually last a long time and rarely need to be replaced

This vehicle has only 30k miles on it and is 10 years old. Look what happens to a vehicle's exhaust system when it is not driven on a regular basis. Rust loves to eat cars that do not move!

I have seen a lot of these systems replaced with custom exhaust systems, in an effort to have the car produce more power and sound a little bit louder. This is real nice and all, but these systems do not usually last as long as the original stainless steel system. These stainless systems come installed on most new model vehicles today.

How long should an exhaust system last? It's entirely dependent on how often you drive the car. If you drive the car at highway speeds and travel thirty minutes to an hour to work every day, it is quite possible that the exhaust system could last as long as you own the vehicle. If you don't drive much and the car just sits in the driveway, especially in a dirt driveway, you could quite possibly replace the exhaust system a couple of times, especially if it is not a stainless steel system. Yes, you can buy a stainless steel custom exhaust system, but you will pay a lot more for it!

Usually any after-market non-stainless steel exhaust system replacement is very inexpensive, because they do not last as long as original factory exhaust systems. You can tell if a non-factory system has been installed simply by recognizing sloppy welding and poorly placed exhaust support hangers. Also, you may notice the exhaust pipe is contacting the underside of the vehicle because it was not routed properly. In this case, you are likely to hear the exhaust hitting on the bottom of the vehicle when you drive the car. The only thing the exhaust system should come into contact with is the exhaust manifold and the rubber support hangers that hold the exhaust system to the bottom of the vehicle.

Identifying Fluid Leaks

Before looking under the vehicle for fluid leaks it's a good idea to pop the hood open and check the fluid levels. If, for example, the power steering fluid reservoir is at its minimum level, then when the vehicle is put on the lift, you would want to focus on the power steering system for leaks. If the coolant reservoir is at minimum level, then you would want to focus on looking for leaks in the cooling system. Do you see what I mean? Okay, let's go!

I want you to focus on the transmission. Look closely where the axle shafts go into the transmission. Make sure there are no signs of fluid loss in this area. If there is fluid loss, it could mean several things. First, it could mean simply that the axle seals are worn and need to be replaced. It could also mean that the transmission may have a restricted transmission breather vent, causing transmission to build up pressure when it gets hot, causing fluid to be pushed out around the axle seals. This could also mean that there is some differential wear, causing a shaft wobble inside the transmission and causing premature failure of the axle seals. In this case, if the transmission had excessive differential wear, it could be a very costly repair—buyer beware!

Pay close attention to the transmission's oil pan gasket sealing area. If you notice transmission fluid leaking from this area, it is usually not a big deal to replace the gasket. However, you will have to drain all the fluid from the transmission to replace this gasket, as pan removal is necessary to replace the gasket. If go so far as to do that, you might as well replace the transmission filter, if it is equipped with one. Please keep in mind that most fluid from an automatic transmission will be red in color. Most fluid in a manual transmission will be brown in color, and if it is gear oil it will smell very strong—quite repulsive, actually!

Let's move to the engine and look for oil loss. Look around the oil pan sealing area, around the oil filter sealing area, and at the oil pan itself for a rust condition. What happens with oil pans is that they get a chip in the paint. From that chip, rust will grow and eventually eat through the oil pan and then cause a leak. If you notice that the car has a rusted oil pan, this can be a costly repair, depending on what you do to replace it! The oil pan itself is not that expensive, but sometimes the labor involved to remove it and replace it can be pricey! Just like the transmission, as we mentioned above, the engine has its own venting system. Sometimes what can happen is that the PCV valve can cause an oil leak if it is not functioning properly. When this PCV valve fails, it can cause crankcase pressures to build up and push oil out past any oil seal in the engine. I have seen complete engine oil seal replacements done only to have them leak oil again, simply because a $10 PCV valve had failed!

Antifreeze Leaks

In previous chapters I have discussed with you the different antifreeze colors. Typically it can be green, but it can be red, blue, or even orange in color. Take a close look underneath the vehicle, toward the very front, and look at the radiator and hoses for signs of leakage there. You especially want to look for leaks if the coolant reservoir or radiator is low on antifreeze. Please be careful not to touch any components involved with the cooling system, as you have just taken the vehicle off the road and components will be hot—so be careful!

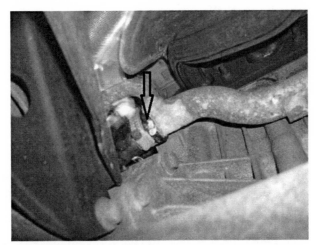

Note the crusty substance; it is dried coolant that over time has leaked past a loose hose clamp.

If you can identify and locate the water pump, it is a good area to look for coolant leaks. On most vehicles today the timing belt drives—or in other words, turns—the water pump, and it is usually under a plastic cover so you cannot see it. In this case, it would be a good idea to find out if the timing belt and water pump have been replaced in the past. If the coolant reservoir is low and you are unable to locate any coolant loss underneath the vehicle, it may be that the coolant level in the reservoir was not topped off at its last service. It is not abnormal for a vehicle to use small amounts of coolant over time. However, if the coolant reservoir is found empty and the radiator fluid level is low, this could be a warning sign that the engine may have a head gasket issue beginning. *Never remove the radiator cap when the engine is warm or hot!* I just want to mention quickly that during the road test, if you are operating the air conditioner, you may see water dripping from the evaporator drain. This is perfectly normal. In fact, this should be the only thing that is dripping from the vehicle.

Power Steering System

Inspecting the power steering system can be a little bit tricky. Sometimes a steering rack can have an internal leak. It will fill the accordion-shaped boots up with power steering fluid at either end of the rack. You may not notice it as an external leak. You could possibly see power steering fluid trying to exit the end of the steering rack through the boots. What happens, in this case, is that the power steering fluid may never have been changed, and consequently the internal seals of the steering rack have been destroyed. Also, dirt may have entered the steering system, causing damage to the seals inside the rack and pinion. The hydraulic lines involved in the system can leak, usually due to rusting, especially here in New England. Power steering fluid can be red in color, as many manufacturers will use automatic transmission fluid to operate their power steering systems. Or it can be brown in color like maple syrup, but a little bit lighter. If the power steering rack is leaking fluid, it can, in most cases, be a labor-intensive process to replace.

Structural Rust

In New England we have a lot of rusty cars, mainly because the amount of salt used on the roads in winter. Also, if you live by the ocean, a vehicle can succumb to the ocean spray laden with salt. If you can actually drive your vehicle on the beach, you are really asking for trouble. You can perfectly maintain your car for the entire time that you own it. Then, you have a little bit of rust start and you don't pay much attention to it, especially if it's underneath where you never see it. It can easily get out of control. One of the best things you can do during the winter months is to bring your car to a car wash and get the salt off as soon as possible.

It's hard to know what the car you are thinking of buying has been exposed to, or whether the person who owned it took care of it with regular car washes, or oil undercoating. Sometimes it does not matter, because some vehicles are notorious for being infested with rust! Simply put, when you are looking underneath the car that you may buy, the less rust, the better! Any rust holes underneath a car will not pass a safety inspection. This includes the rocker panels that run on the left and right sides of the vehicle. Make sure that you open each door and look at the bottoms of the doors for rust. When the bottoms of doors rust out, this is usually caused by the door drains being restricted due to debris. Thus, water does not drain out the bottom of the doors.

Brake Lines and Fuel Lines

Depending on the manufacturer of a car or truck, brake lines or fuel lines can be very costly to replace. Some manufacturers, mostly Asian-manufactured vehicles, use stainless steel or coated brake or fuel lines that usually last the lifetime of a vehicle. Many domestic automakers, in the past, used the least expensive brake and fuel lines in their vehicles. It did not take long for them to rust and leak, especially in New England. American automakers are sure to increase the quality of their products to rebuild confidence in the American consumer. I have already seen increased quality in the brake lines and fuel lines that come equipped in American vehicles. Let's keep up the good work, America!

Make sure the vehicle you're thinking of purchasing does not have excessively rusty brake or fuel lines. If the brake lines and fuel lines are just starting to show indications of rust, you can slow this process down by spraying a combination of rust penetrate and spray grease to the fuel lines and brake lines. If you do need to have brake lines replaced, you can purchase coated or stainless steel replacement lines that will last much longer. It does cost a little more, but it is worth it in the long run. If you do have a brake line or fuel line fail and you decide to replace only the brake line or fuel line that failed, please be aware that there may be more leaking lines soon to follow. Brake lines do not rust only from the outside; they can also be eaten away from the inside, due to excessive moisture in the brake fluid. This is another important reason that brake fluid replacement needs to be done periodically. I will cover this in the maintenance section of this book.

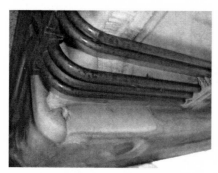 

Note that these brake and fuel lines on the left are coated and should never rust or leak. The brake lines on the right are not coated lines and are badly rusted and starting to leak.

Wheels and Tires

While you have the vehicle on a hoist, it is a good idea to give each wheel a spin, to check to see if the tire is out of round or a wheel is bent. It does not take that much of a bend in a rim to feel a vibration driving down the road. It does not take much to make a tire out of round or out of balance. A low-quality tire may take a lot of weight to balance it. You may never get all of the vibration out of the tire or wheel, because of this. Also, you can see how easily the wheel will spin. There should not be any excessive drag on any of the wheels. You will have a little bit of drag from the wheels which have axles. If you have excessive drag from the wheels, this could indicate that the wheels are dragging and that the brakes may need servicing or replacing. Please make sure that the vehicle is in neutral; otherwise, the wheels will be difficult to spin. This is also the time to get a good look at how much tread is left on the tires and how the tires are wearing. Make sure that all the tires are the same size, as well. This really makes it easy to get a straightforward look at the tires without actually removing the wheels from the car.

Note the wear bars that are highlighted white with a tire crayon.
This tire needs to be discarded.

Suspension Components

I will not go into great detail about how to inspect suspension components, because this needs to be done by a professional mechanic. However, I will give you a description of suspension components that need to be inspected by a professional for your safety. The components are as follows: *ball joints, tie rod ends, wheel bearings, coil and leaf springs struts, idler arms and stabilizer links, if equipped. Control arms and bushings need to be checked as well.* If any or all of these components are found loose, they need to be replaced before you purchase the vehicle. The vehicle should not pass any safety inspection with loose or broken suspension components. Make sure that if any suspension components are to be replaced, that only high-quality parts are used.

Some manufacturers, like Moog, carry a lifetime warranty on their suspension parts. Keep in mind that if you are buying the vehicle from a dealership, they are likely to try to use the cheapest parts available to keep costs down and profits up! Another thing I want you to remember is that when you are on a road test, if you hear a clunking noise from the front or rear of the car, it may be only stabilizer bar bushings. Many repair shops may not properly diagnose a suspension complaint. The first thing they try to sell you is a set of struts. I have seen people needlessly spend hundreds of dollars replacing struts, when the source of the noise was only an inexpensive pair of stabilizer bushings or stabilizer links!

Remember—open your eyes, but only with safety glasses on!

CHAPTER 8
Financing

You need some capital to purchase your used or new car. Or maybe you have all the money saved up—if so, good for you! If you are currently still in high school and are taking a driver's education class, hopefully you have been saving your pennies working a part-time job after school to have some kind of down payment. Just maybe you are one of the lucky ones, and ever since you were born, your parents have been tucking money away for you for college and a car to get you back and forth safely. If not, hopefully you DO have some money set aside for a good down payment, if you are thinking about financing your first car.

Without having any credit established, you might need a co-signer to help you establish credit and get a decent down payment. The co-signer might be your parents, but truthfully you should try to swing it on your own. Unfortunately, these days most schools do not teach financial literacy. With that said, if you are just starting off on the journey of life, you need to learn early about the difference between an asset and a liability. The worst thing you can do is to start out in this world with a car that has a big payment and one that will plague you with repair bills. It is all about due diligence on your part, so be very methodical in your search for a good used car. Obviously this approach will work for anyone. Even if you have owned many cars, you should still use this approach.

Banks today may not be so willing to lend you 100% of any amount of money, big or small, especially for a used vehicle. You can start by looking through your phone book at all the banks and start calling and asking what their current interest rates are for a used car loan. You will find that the interest rates are much higher for a used car than for a new one. Please take into consideration that when you drive your new or used car off the lot, the car will automatically depreciate **20%** to **30%** as soon as you drive it off the lot! In other words, if you buy a car for **$30,000** it will possibly drop in value **$9,000** when you drive it home for the first time. Of course, a lot of this relies on who manufactured the vehicle, and resale value.

You should not take a car loan for more than three years. You need to set money aside to properly maintain the vehicle, so that you can drive the car many years after the car is paid for. If you have to finance a car for four to five years, the car is too expensive for you. If you are strapped for cash, you should not be buying a new car. You should find a good dependable used car that you can afford. Remember, cars do not appreciate in value. They depreciate. If you have a desirable classic car, this may be a different story. When you buy a home it will appreciate as the years go by, if you invest money and time by making improvements to the home. It would be great if this were true with automobiles—however, it is not! Research vehicles that hold their trade-in value the best, and try for them.

After three years go by and your car is paid for, you should strive to keep it for an additional three to five years at least. You should still make that car payment to yourself after your car is paid for. If you have what it takes to discipline yourself and put that money away for three years, you will have a great down payment for your next car. It may be hard for you at first to do this, but once you get in the habit of saving that car payment for yourself, it's a great feeling. Just imagine that you had a $300 car payment and you tucked that money away for three years for yourself. That would be $10,800 for you! Not a bad down payment for a new car, wouldn't you agree? This is called getting more bang for your buck!

It has been my practice, when shopping for a used car loan, to make my local credit union my last stop. I have seen that most banks cannot come close to the low rates that a credit union offers for a used car loan. In most cases, you will have to open an account at the credit union before they will think of lending you any money. Let's say the car you are looking at purchasing is $5,000. If you do not have all of the money saved, you are obviously going to have to get some help. You should have at least half of that amount saved up—in this case, it would be $2,500. get some help. You should have at least half of that amount saved up—in this case, it would be $2,500. Your best bet is to have all the money saved up to buy your first used car. You could always muster up the courage to ask your parents if they will co- sign on the loan for you, but that usually is not a good idea!

Of course, this depends on what kind of relationship you have with your parents, but I am sure they will be proud of you if you do it on your own. You need to realize that if you don't make your car pay-ment, or you are late on a payment, that directly affects your parents' good credit in a bad way! We do not want to start the journey of life on the wrong foot, do we? Just a friendly reminder—whatever your monthly payment will be, don't forget to add what it is going to cost to register, insure, and inspect the vehicle. Last but not least, don't forget to factor in what it is going to cost to maintain the vehicle over the time you plan on owning it. Do your homework and see what the annual cost of ownership has historically been for the vehicle you are thinking of purchasing. You do not want to buy a money pit!

One very important thing you have to be careful of is not to get upside down in the vehicle. This means you do not want to owe more than what the car is worth. If you do this, are pretty much stuck with the vehicle until you get it paid for, and at that point the vehicle will be worthless to anyone. What happened? Somebody didn't do their homework to look at a certain vehicle's historic track record, as far as dependability, and annual cost of maintenance and ownership. What they usually see is a sporty, shiny red car. They just have to have that car and they don't usually try to haggle with the price because they want the car so much! They pay near full retail for the vehicle, and they don't get any kind of extended warranty. Then the unexpected surprises pop up.

Let me give you a made-up example. This kind of thing happens all the time. Billy is looking for a used car and he drives by a dealership and sees a nice little car. Let's say this car is red. One of his buddies basically has the same car but it is blue. It's a year older than the one he is looking at. He knows that his friend wanted a red car, so Billy has to have this car to try to make his friend jealous and impress him at the same time. He pulls into the dealership with his parents' car, comes to a stop, gets out of the car, and starts walking around the red car. Little does he know a salesman spotted him pulling into the dealership and is now walking toward him hastily before he gets away. The salesman just so happens to have the key to the car with the dealer plate. He says, "Hey, buddy—you want to take it for a spin?" Billy says, "Sure!" The rest is history!

Billy purchases the red car. His friend with the blue car is momentarily jealous that Billy has the red car that he wanted, but that is about it! Next thing you know Billy is getting bombarded with repair bills, and he has a monthly car payment to boot! He has not set any money aside for unexpected surprises. He will soon be in an impossible situation and become upside down in the vehicle with no real way out. I have seen people do this more than once with all makes and models of vehicle. If you must learn the hard way, so be it! People who buy and sell cars frequently are often unconsciously compensating for low self-esteem issues. Most people do not connect who you are with what you drive. They just don't care, so get over it! I strongly advise that you do your homework. Find out what the cost of ownership is for the vehicle that you are thinking of purchasing, and how it holds its trade in value down the road.

Extended Warranties

If you are offered an extended warranty, in most cases it may not be a bad idea, especially if the vehicle you are thinking of purchasing has a track record of needing extensive and expensive repairs. My focus in this book is for you to avoid buying a money pit. I would strongly advise that you do your homework. Call your local shops to see what regular repair bills may be for a similar year, make, and model of the vehicle you are thinking of purchasing. A salesperson will more than likely offer you an extended warranty toward the end of the sale. If the salesperson is real pushy about the warranty, he or she may know something about the car that they don't want to tell you about. They just want to make the sale, and if the problem arises after you purchase the car, they can just simply say, "Oh, don't worry—that's covered under the warranty you purchased." Ask for a copy of the warranty for you to review, **so you can see exactly what the warranty will cover or not cover.**

I recommend if that if you decide to purchase an extended warranty on a used car, it should cover the engine, transmission, driveline, and axles. You may finance the cost of the warranty into your payment, if you choose to buy the warranty policy. Over the years I have heard salespeople joking, while watching a customer leave the parking lot with their new to them used car, saying, "There they go with their tail light warranty!" In other words, after they see your tail lights go away, so does your warranty! With that said, in some cases it may not be a bad idea for you to purchase an extended warranty and finance it into your monthly payment. If you do not purchase the warranty, just make sure that you have some money tucked away for any surprises that may pop up in the future. Remember, when we purchase something, we are driven by 95% emotion and only 5% thought—think about it!

Leasing a Car

In my opinion, leasing a car is foolish. Do not do it, unless you plan on doing it for the rest of your life and never really owning a car. *Think about it seriously! It has to be an ideal situation for it to be worthwhile.* If you are the type of person who knows exactly how many miles you are going to drive in any given year, a lease may be for you. If you are okay paying for a car three years and never owning it, go for it. If you do decide to lease a car, you will get a new car every three years, and some love the idea behind that. I have never leased a vehicle, nor do I intend to. What do you expect from a guy who is forty-five years old, and has owned only seven cars! I have known people who have leased a car for three years, and liked the car so much then they bought out the lease. The problem with that is you end up paying way too much for the car. Not for me. Depending on the vehicle that you lease, and if your mileage comes in lower than expected, the dealer may owe you for that at the end of the lease. Read any and all contracts carefully before signing them.

A Quick Note About Classic Cars

Let's say a 1965 Ford Mustang convertible is driving down the road. The car is absolutely stunning! Instantly, you're fantasizing about being behind the wheel of that classic car. If you do purchase one of these classic cars, you had better plan to work on the car yourself, or have more than enough money set aside to have somebody else work on it for you. Even if the car has been completely restored and is in mint condition, it still takes a lot of money and time to keep the car that way, especially a classic car.

You also have to take into consideration that you will not be driving this car in the winter months. You will need another car to get you through the winter months. From a financial standpoint, this could get very costly! If you want a classic car that badly, you had better think about it thoroughly. If you are seriously considering purchasing a classic car, ask if it has been appraised. If it has been appraised, ask to see the appraisal and see if it coincides with the asking price. As far as pricing and classic cars are concerned, a strong or weak economy greatly affects the price of the vehicle.

In a nutshell: Don't do anything foolish. If you think you really want a certain car, put a refundable deposit and a hold tag on it. Think about it thoroughly for a couple days or a week, before you make any hasty decisions. Make sure you can afford it! A little thought will pay off in a large way before you purchase a classic car of any make or model.

We Owe Slip

You are going to pick up your new/used car today and you have done all your homework and gotten a great deal. Good for you! You sit down with your salesperson and finish up some paperwork, and you cannot wait to drive your car home and show it off. The salesperson tells you that the parts department forgot to order the fog lights that were promised to you. He did get the order in, but the fog lights are on national back order and they won't be in for three weeks. He verbally promises you (nothing in writing) that when the fog lights arrive, he will call you and make the necessary arrangements to have the service department install the fog lights. Well, three weeks and a day go by and you have heard no word of your fog lights arriving, so you call the dealership and ask to speak with your salesperson. You are then told that the salesperson who sold you your car no longer works there, and left without notice. You then ask to speak to the sales manager and he checks into it and states that the fog lights did not get ordered and he apologizes. He then says, "Just show me the We Owe slip, and we will take care of you." Guess what—you never got a We Owe slip from the salesperson who quit his job! This scenario is just one of many things that can be promised to you and not delivered to you. The day that you pick up your car, make sure that you have a We Owe slip made out for you if they OWE you something for your car!

Make doubly sure that the car has everything it car came with new, such as a jack, spare tire, and tools. If the car does not have an owner's manual in the glove box, make sure they put that on the We Owe slip as well.

What you may encounter when trading in your car

Let's say that you want to purchase a brand new car. You have done all of your homework and you found the car that suites your needs. Your old car has treated you well and you have a stack of maintenance records to fall back on to justify what you would like to see shown for trade in value. You searched the web Kelley blue book. com, Edmunds.com to get trade in value for your car. For example we are going to say your vehicle has 140,000 miles on it and it is 7 years old and the trade in value is $6,900. You now find yourself at the dealership driving the car you want and you are at the table talking numbers with the sales person. Then the question is asked to you, "How much are you looking to get for your trade"? You say $6,900, at that point the salesperson says I will have to go talk to my manager about that. He leaves you for a short time and comes back and says, "We can only show you $4,000 for your trade towards your new car, because that is what we will probably get at auction for it. You need to be prepared for this to happen. Not only do you need to get the trade in value, but you also need to find what your particular vehicle is bringing in for money at auction before you bring your vehicle in to trade it. I suggest that you make some random phone calls to dealerships in your area to ask what a vehicle like yours is selling for at auction, or search the web obviously. They may not give you those numbers so you may want to ask it another way. Ask what the cash value is for your car. You need to get as close as you can get to trade in value for your old car, be persistent.

CHAPTER 9
Vital Fluids and Maintenance

My shop teacher in high school instructed me about the importance of servicing your vehicle to make it last a long time. Most importantly, changing the fluids in your car on a regular basis is key. It only makes sense. If you purchase a used vehicle from a dealership or a reputable used car facility, you should only have to do regular oil changes, check your tire pressures, and rotate your tires for the first year you own it. This will hold true especially if the vehicle has been a certified used car.

It also depends on you as an individual. Years ago when I worked at a Honda dealership there was a customer who did every service that Honda recommended. However, the customer was not exactly a neat freak. Every time the customer brought the vehicle in for service, it was pretty much a pig sty. The customer had so many children that it was hard to keep the vehicle clean. I am not kidding. When the customer brought the vehicle in for service, there would be half-eaten apple cores on the floor, coffee mugs, dirty laundry, and the occasional vomit on the door panel. If you have children, you know that it is hard to keep your car clean. I sure do. But come on! The customer said on several occasions they expected to get top dollar trade-in value for the Honda Odyssey. The customer based this expectation primarily on the fact the vehicle was serviced regularly and had all the records to prove it! Mechanically, the vehicle was fairly sound, but it did not help the fact that the customer lived on a dirt road. The vehicle was exposed to the annual mud season, which shows no mercy to a vehicle over time.

When the customer was ready to trade the vehicle in, it was not in the greatest of shape. The sales department could not get the carpet clean and sent the vehicle to auction anyway. It is important to keep your car clean and well-maintained throughout the years, to keep its value.

I had a disagreement once with a co-worker at an independent shop I worked at. It was a busy day at the shop and I was unable to service a vehicle I previously recommended preventative maintenance to. The service advisor had no choice but to give the car to him to work on. In so many words, he told me that he did not agree with me as to how I recommended fluid replacement in vehicles. *He told me that he did not believe in it.* He basically told me that I was changing fluids too soon and they should be changed only when the fluid gets black, or dirty. I quickly ended the conversation, as it could easily have led to an argument. As he neared retirement, he had never asked himself, "Why am I replacing this transmission? Why did this wheel cylinder fail? How come this power steering rack is leaking?" The reasons for all these mechanical failures can be traced back to the fact that he never looked at the condition and color of the fluid for the failed component. CHANGE THE FLUID BEFORE IT GETS TOO OLD AND DIRTY! It is not rocket science. What would you rather pay for, a $200 transmission fluid exchange, or a $1,500 to $3,000 or more automatic transmission replacement? I think the answer is obvious.

In the past I have been criticized by co-workers for what I have recommended for service to customers' vehicles. I never have and never will recommend services or maintenance to someone prematurely. The services that I recommend to customers for their cars are the same services I perform on my own cars. That is my standard of recommended maintenance, period.

The Importance of Exchanging Your Vehicle's Vital Fluids

Having dependable, reliable, and safe transportation for you and your family is a must. Having your engine's oil and filter changed on a regular basis is an important first step to proper maintenance of your vehicle for a long life of dependability. Another very important factor is the remaining fluids in your car. These vital fluids need to be checked every oil and filter service—not just the level of the fluids, but the condition of the fluids. The trick here is to exchange your fluids before they get too dirty. If you purchased your car new, in most cases, fluids start to darken in color around 30,000 to 40,000 miles. Most component failure is due to excessive heat. As a fluid gets older and dirtier, its ability to remove heat is greatly reduced. Any fluid in your vehicle is important to replace before it gets too dirty and basically worn-out.

Brake Fluid

One of the most important and neglected fluids in vehicles today is brake fluid. Brake fluid is hygroscopic. This means it attracts moisture easily. New brake fluid has a boiling point right around 450 degrees F. When moisture is introduced to brake fluid over time, it greatly reduces the brake fluid's effectiveness to transmit the pressure that you are applying from the brake pedal to each wheel needed to stop the vehicle. When brake fluid contains over 2% moisture content, it is a good time to think about exchanging it for new fluid. There are vehicles on the road right now with 10+-year-old fluid in them!

Typically, every two years you should exchange your brake fluid.

When brake fluid has too much moisture in it and it gets too hot, it will boil. When brake fluid boils it aerates the fluid with tiny air bubbles and causes your brake pedal to fade or become spongy. Old brake fluid and too much moisture can eat away at the copper lining inside the brake line. This can shorten the life of other components in your car's braking system, such as master cylinders, wheel cylinders and caliper piston seals. Remember, when you have your car serviced, your brake fluid level should not be topped off. You need to know why the brake fluid level is low. When you have had a brake job done, it is always best to replace your brake fluid at the same time.

Hydraulic Clutch Fluid

Most vehicles today with a manual transmission have the clutch operated with a hydraulic system. This means instead of a cable connecting your clutch pedal to the clutch arm on your transmission, it is controlled hydraulically via a clutch master cylinder, and then a metal line to a slave cylinder at the transmission. This fluid is actually brake fluid, and should be exchanged for the same reasons as mentioned above. Changing this fluid is easy, and it will greatly decrease the chance for costly clutch master or slave cylinder failure.

Power Steering Fluid

Here is another neglected fluid in today's vehicles. Power steering fluid is another hydraulic fluid that is important to exchange. Changing this fluid will extend the life of your power steering pump and the seals in your power steering rack. New fluid will remove heat from the system more efficiently than the old fluid. It is a good idea to keep the fluid clean in the power steering system. Excessive temperatures, due to high pressure in the power steering system, can damage seals in the rack as well as cause premature damage to the pump.

When power steering fluid darkens, this can actually be caused by the deterioration of the various seals from excessive heat and pressure in the system. Thus, it is important to change this fluid before it changes color, every 15,000 miles. Some vehicles use automatic transmission fluid. Some use standard power steering fluid. Some European and Asian vehicles use a specialty fluid. It is important that the auto repair shop you choose uses the correct fluid for your power steering system, otherwise you could end up with a leaking system due to using the incorrect fluid. Simply exchanging this fluid is much less costly than replacing your steering rack or power steering pump.

Automatic Transmission Fluid

It is very important that your automatic transmission fluid level and condition is checked at every oil change. The key to having your transmission last for the life of your car is to have the old fluid exchanged for new. If you only have your transmission fluid drained and refilled, you are not replacing all the fluid. Much of the old fluid is still in the torque converter. The torque converter is a large round component that is connected between the engine and transmission pump. If you change your transmission fluid before it gets too dirty, several drain and refills may be acceptable, in some cases.

Most automatic transmissions that have replaceable filters should be replaced when you have a fluid exchange performed on your vehicle. If your transmission has bands that are adjustable, they should be adjusted upon fluid exchange.

For a vehicle that is exposed to severe conditions such as heavy towing or plowing, you may want to exchange your fluid annually. Remember this: Too much heat destroys a transmission. Dirty automatic transmission fluid does not remove heat as well as new, clean transmission fluid. Keep your fluid changed at least every 30,000 miles or sooner if exposed to severe conditions.

Transfer Case Fluid

The transfer case is used in most four-wheel drive vehicles. It does just that—it transfers power to the front wheels when you activate your four-wheel drive.

This fluid gets worn out with time and usage, and should be changed when your transmission fluid is exchanged. In most cases, this fluid is just drained and refilled, with minimal labor involved.

Front and Rear Differential Fluids

Vehicles with front and rear differentials—mostly four-wheel drive trucks—have gear oils that need to be replaced. This also is usually a drain and refill process that involves minimal labor and can save you so much money down the road. You can reference your owner's manual to try to determine when your differential fluids need to be replaced; however, inspecting the fluid is the best way to see if it is time to replace the fluid. If you tow a trailer or camper or transport heavy loads, you will definitely want to replace this fluid sooner than later! If the rear differential fluid gets too dirty, it can actually overheat the axle seals, harden them, and cause them to leak and ruin your brake shoes, which can be very costly down the road. So a simple drain and refill can not only extend the life of your carrier, pinion, and axle bearings, but it could quite possibly save you from an unexpected brake job in the future. Most drain plugs for rear differentials have a magnet on them to catch any metal that the plug might attract. If your drain plug has excessive metal clinging to it, the rear differential cover should be removed to inspect gears and bearings for excessive wear. Front and rear differentials have vents that need to be checked for restrictions. If these vents are restricted, pressure can build up in the differential and axle, and pinion seals can leak prematurely.

Antifreeze/Engine Coolant

Your vehicle's engine's longevity relies on how effectively your coolant can remove heat from your engine. It is formulated to protect and lubricate internal components of your engine's cooling system, such as your water pump. Your car also relies on this fluid to keep the cooling system from freezing solid in the winter and severely damaging the engine. As this fluid gets older, the various compounds or silicates do not stay in suspension as they were designed to do, and settle to the bottom of your engine's cooling system. Obviously the fluid should be changed before it gets to this point. You should have it checked at every oil change. The coolant reservoir bottle should always be kept at the maximum level.

Antifreeze starts out alkaline when it is new; as it gets older, it will turn acidic. When your antifreeze is in this acidic state, it tends to be corrosive to the internal components of your cooling system. It is important to replace your antifreeze before it turns acidic. Usually a 50/50 mix will bring your antifreeze protection to -40 F. That is where you want it to be. It is very important that distilled water is used to mix your coolant. If you use tap water, it can cause excessive internal corrosion of your engine's cooling system, due to high mineral content in the water. Understand that if antifreeze is overprotected—let's say to -60F—the antifreeze can work against you. It can actually gel up and not flow as it should. If it is too weak, your engine can freeze in the winter months. If the coolant is too weak it can also not remove heat to cool the engine in the summer months.

Engine Oil and Filter Changes

Don't wait too long between oil changes. Your engine's oil will get too thin, mostly due to unburned fuel getting past the piston rings into the crank case. If you do not have your air filter checked or replaced on a regular basis, guess where the dirt goes? That's right, into your engine's oil! Oh, sure; the oil filter will do the best it can to filter this dirt and grime out, until it is overwhelmed with grime, and then it will all go right through the filter into your engine's bearings. After about 5,000 miles, oil will bypass the dirty oil filter and no longer be cleaned as it would when the filter was new. Do not buy the cheapest oil filter available! Sooner or later you will be replacing your engine, simply due to lack of proper maintenance with simple oil and filter changes. Remember—no oil, your car no move!

Synthetic engine oil costs a little bit more than conventional motor oil, but if you plan on owning your vehicle for a long time, I recommend that you use it. In my personal vehicles I use synthetic motor oil and go 5,000 miles between oil and filter changes. I check my fluids every thousand miles or so, along with my tire pressures. Even if your vehicle comes equipped with tire pressure monitors, it is a good idea to check your tires with a trusty old tire gauge occasionally. Depending on the vehicle if all four tires were to lose 10 psi (pounds per square inch) equally, the warning light for the TPMS (tire pressure monitoring system) might never illuminate.

If you buy a vehicle with higher mileage on it, you should not use synthetic oil, if for most of the vehicle's life it had primarily conventional oil used. The reason I do not recommend this is because synthetic oil can loosen sludge in the engine and could possibly block crucial oil passages, causing engine failure.

Engines that come equipped with a turbo should use synthetic oil from day one. A turbo spins at a very high RPM. The bearings in the turbo need synthetic oil to get the maximum lifespan from the turbo. If you are thinking of buying a used car that has a turbocharged engine, you need to find out from the previous owner if they used synthetic oil, and when they changed their oil. If they don't know or they did not use synthetic oil and you buy the car, you may end up replacing the turbo prematurely. If you do decide to buy a vehicle that has a turbo-charged engine, just make sure that you use synthetic oil for every oil change. It is also a good idea to let your engine idle for a few minutes after you have been driving it to allow the turbo to cool down properly. Check your owner's manual for information pertaining to turbo cool-down time.

Before you buy a car that has a turbo-charged engine, call the dealership or local independent shop. Get an estimate as to what it may cost to replace the turbo. You may want to sit down when they tell you how much!

If you are to stick with conventional motor oil, I recommend that you replace the engine oil and filter every 3000 to 4000 miles, or three to four months. I will say this again because I feel it is worth mentioning again and again. *Check all of your fluid levels and condition regularly, along with your tire pressures!*

CHAPTER 10
Finding a Good Mechanic

This automotive technician knows what tool he needs
and where to find it every time.

I t is important that you find a good mechanic: one that makes you
feel confident with the repairs or service that he or she has done
for you. You want to know that your wheel lug nuts have been properly tightened! This book is not just about getting your car fixed
properly. It is about the experience that you, the customer, should

receive. How long did you have to wait before your car was brought into the shop? Was the repair estimate accurate or close to your actual repair bill? If not, was the bill explained to you in detail? Was your car washed or vacuumed when you picked it up, as promised? Was your car easy to find in the parking lot? Was it backed into the parking spot so you could easily drive straight out? Was there a paper floor mat on the floor? If you answered no to any of these questions, you may want to rethink the service experience that you have been receiving. Many of the things I just mentioned are not all the mechanic's responsibility. In most cases, the mechanic can be only as good as the service manager or service advisor who handed your keys over to your mechanic. You wouldn't give a waitress a bad tip because the chef overcooked your steak, would you?

You need to know the difference between a parts replacer and an automotive technician. Simply stated, a parts replacer will replace a part on your car, cross his fingers, and hope it fixes your car. The automotive technician will perform diagnostic procedures with almost the same approach every time and with the same results every time. When an automotive technician diagnoses a failed component, he will determine why the component failed and will do what it takes to prevent the new component from failing prematurely.

An experienced automotive technician will implement a protocol that I like to refer as the three V'S. First, he must "Verify" your complaint with a road test. Second, he must "Verify" a repair for the problem. Then third, he must "Verify" that he has fixed the problem with proper road test. When I say a proper road test, I mean at least a five-mile road test or more, to confirm that the vehicle has been repaired and will not inconvenience the customer by needing to come back with the same problem again. The typical parts replacer will not take the time to analyze why a particular component failed. Let me give you an example.

A vehicle is towed in to a shop and the customer complains that they were driving along and their car suddenly lost power and stalled like it ran out of fuel. The parts replacer finds the car is not getting fuel, so it must need a fuel pump. He verifies that the fuel pump is getting power needed to run the pump, so suspects the fuel pump is bad and he orders a fuel pump. He then replaces the fuel pump. The car runs and drives; the customer pays the bill and is momentarily happy because their car is on the road again. The customer drives their car for one hundred miles or so, and the same thing happens—the car acts like it has run out of fuel. The car is towed back to the shop and the same mechanic gets the car, scratches his head, and says, "It must be a defective fuel pump." He replaces the fuel pump again; the customer drives the car for about the same distance, and guess what? You guessed it—the fuel pump fails again. Frustrated, the customer has their car towed to another shop and has an automotive technician diagnose the problem. He finds that the fuel pump indeed was bad because the vehicle had the original fuel filter and it was badly restricted, causing the fuel pump to overwork and fail prematurely. This cause and effect can happen with many systems in a vehicle, and can be easily avoided with a little thought and proper procedure.

It would not be fair if I did not defend my fellow automotive technicians out there by stating that it is not always the technician's fault if the vehicle is repaired incorrectly. Let me give you a scenario that will help you to understand. One day a customer brings their car in and complains that they hear a groaning-type noise from the rear of their vehicle at highway speeds. Gary, the auto technician, road tests the vehicle, brings the car into the shop, and verifies that the car has a noisy right rear wheel bearing. Gary then goes to the parts department and gets price and availability for a right rear wheel bearing for said vehicle. Unfortunately, the wheel bearing is not in stock and must be ordered. The part is ordered and the customer reschedules an appointment for the following week to have the wheel bearing replaced. The customer drops the car off to have the bearing replaced, but a couple of things happen. The service advisor or dispatcher does not give the job to Gary, the original technician who diagnosed the car; the car is given to Sam, who did not diagnose the car.

Sam reads the repair order and it says "Replace *the left rear wheel bearing.*" Sam then replaces the left rear wheel bearing and he drives the car and notices that there still is a noisy wheel bearing from the right rear. What happened? Total communication failure; that is what happened. Somewhere along the line, someone dropped the ball, so to speak, and dispatched the job to a mechanic who did not diagnose the vehicle—and "left rear wheel bearing" was printed on the repair order, when "right rear wheel bearing" should have been printed on the repair order. As I stated at the beginning of this chapter, the mechanic can only be as good as the first person the customer talks to, which is the service advisor or manager. There are so many variables that can affect the performance or efficiency of an automotive technician—so when your car is not ready as promised, do not be so quick to point a finger at your mechanic.

You should look for a mechanic that is or has been ASE (Automotive Service Excellence) Certified. ASE is a nationally recognized certification for automotive and truck technicians. It is also beneficial if the establishment that you take your vehicle to allows you to talk directly to the mechanic who works on your car. This holds true especially if the service advisor does not explain to your satisfaction what was done to your car—or what needs to be done, for that matter. Often the service advisor can act as a filter between you and the technician. You may not get the whole story as to what your car needs for repairs or service.

You also need to find a mechanic who does not mind talking to customers.

If you see a shop advertising a $9.95 special for an oil change service, keep on driving! If you are lured into a shop like this, prepare to get a lot of stuff sold to you that you may or may not need for your car. You see, $9.95 does not even pay for the oil and filter. They have to sell you something to make money. If you do happen to go into a shop like this, ask for an itemized list of anything that may need attention on your car.

Call automotive repair shops in the area. Get estimates for the repair work you are told you need. If they find something that is a safety-related item, have them explain to you what danger this could pose, if you do not make the repairs that day. If they give you a logical explanation as to why you need to do this repair and give you competitive estimates, by all means have the repair done. Yes, even if it means you pay a little more for it, you may want to have the repair done for you that day, especially if your safety is in jeopardy. Don't forget to ask for or see the old parts. If you are shopping around for good service for your car, ask if you can take a tour of their shop. If you are able to take a guided tour of the shop and it is a mess, you should probably keep shopping for good service! A messy, disorganized shop usually means that messy, disorganized work will be performed on your car.

You want to find a shop that is well-organized and neat. You want to find a mechanic who cleans up his tools at the end of the day. You want to find a mechanic who does not just leave all his tools in a huge pile on the bench at the end of the workday. Guess who pays for the lost time a mechanic spends looking through that pile of tools for a wrench? That's right, you do! Through the years, I have worked alongside some real disorganized mechanics in the auto repair business. It seems these guys waste more time looking around for tools, than they spend working on cars. You may also be able to count on one of these mechanics to leave the grease smudge on your carpet or your paint! It happens—mechanics get greasy; that's what we do! Your mechanic may not notice that he left a smudge behind on your car. If this does happen to you, just go back to the shop and tell them about it and they should gladly remove the grease smudge for you.

Safety Inspections

There is a big difference between having a safety inspection performed and getting a "sticka" slapped on your windshield. For those of you who are not from the New England area, "sticka" means state inspection sticker here (to some people). A proper safety inspection should take about 30 to 45 minutes. It should take much longer for large trucks. I am unable to tell you how many times it has happened that someone will wait until the very last minute to get the safety inspection done on their car. It is usually the procrastinators, who do little or nothing to their cars, who come in and say, "I need a sticker or I'm going to get pulled over and get fined!" They will look for a shop that will basically check the lights on the car, and if it passes emissions inspection, then they get their sticker! This type of individual is not really concerned whether their car is safe or not, or whether they are a risk to themselves or other motorists on the road. All they care about is not getting pulled over for an expired state inspection sticker.

Many times a car comes in for service, which just passed a safety inspection a month prior, and it needs tires, windshield wipers, or brakes. I make notes about this to inform the customers. Some customers are pleased that I have found these items, and others are not so happy, because these items were not found during their car's safety inspection. I have had customers who really don't care, or wait until it breaks, and then they will fix it … as cheaply as possible, too! Some vehicles that come into the shop from a state that do not have a mandatory safety inspection truly scare me. I have strongly suggested suspension repair or tire replacement on some of these vehicles, and the customer declines because the state they come from does not require a safety inspection. But it's okay for them to drive their unsafe car in a state that requires a safety inspection? Doesn't make a whole lot of sense. If the state that you live in does not require them, please take my advice and get a proper safety inspection performed on your own by your mechanic—do it for yourself, your family, and everyone you share the road with.

Just two baby seats? No, those are two precious cargo carriers!
Get a complete and trusted safety inspection.

You need to find a shop that does a complete thorough safety inspection, one that will actually remove your wheels and inspect the brakes—a shop that notices the all-important baby seat in the back of your car.

Word-of-mouth can be one of the best ways to find a used car. Word-of-mouth can also be one of the best ways to find a good mechanic. If you are new to the area, ask one of your co-workers, or a family member, who they use for auto repair and service. If you can find a good, honest mechanic, he is worth his weight in gold to you! Use common sense and trust your intuition when looking for a good mechanic!

Understanding the Flat-Rate Pay System

What does the mechanic's flat-rate pay system have to do with this chapter on finding a good mechanic? A lot, actually—it is important that you understand the flat-rate pay system that most auto repair shops and automotive dealerships use today. What I am about to tell you may seem like I am not on your side at first blush, but I *am* on your side; that is why I am writing this book. Since its introduction over the years, the flat-rate pay system has gotten a bad reputation. I feel that I need to explain to you how it works. Most people do not understand it. When they get a brief explanation of it, they feel like they are getting ripped off. It can depend on where you bring your car for service—an honest shop, or one that is not so honest. You need to know that you are getting what you paid for.

If the posted labor rate is $75 per hour at an automotive repair shop, this does not mean that the mechanic makes $75 per hour. Most mechanics, where I come from in the northeast, are lucky if they make $18 to $20 per hour in the year 2011. I am still amazed, to this day, how many people believe that mechanics make the posted labor rate. It used to be that a mechanic made half of the posted labor rate. Those days are long since past. Keep in mind that most of the time, an automotive technician today holds a thankless job. It is both physically and mentally challenging on a daily basis. There is a good chance that the mechanic who worked on your car may have gotten injured in some way during the process of repairing your car.

Basically, the flat-rate pay system is designed to increase productivity within the shop. It also gives the mechanic a much better paycheck and increases the mechanic's incentive to produce work. In a well-managed and organized shop, the system can be to your benefit. It offers you more accurate repair estimates, and the repair work gets done in a timely manner. However, in a poorly managed and disorganized shop, it may not be such a good thing.

Each labor operation has a certain amount of time allowed to perform the work on a car. For example, if your car needs front brakes, the labor time is 2.5 hours to replace the front brake rotors and brake pads. The technician brings your car into the shop and replaces your front brakes in 1.8 hours. The technician will get paid 2.5 hours of time, even though it took him only 1.8 hours to perform the job. If it takes the mechanic 4.0 hours to do the job, he still gets paid only for the 2.5 hours. If the mechanic does a poor job and you come back with a complaint—perhaps he left one of the caliper bolts loose—he will need to correct the issue on his own time. Many things can affect the mechanic's performance in a negative way, as far as flat rate is concerned. If the mechanic loses time because the wrong parts showed up, or the wrong parts were supplied by the customer, the mechanic will usually eat the lost time.

An experienced automotive technician will be allowed a specific amount of time to perform each labor task that is presented to him or her, and may or may not beat the flat-rate time in the first round. If the mechanic is handed the same procedure on the same type of vehicle the following day, the mechanic will obviously do the job faster and more efficiently. This is when the mechanic is rewarded for his or her efficiency.

If you have a service or repair done on your car that is supposed to take 3.0 hours to perform and the mechanic gets it done in 1 hour, you may want to question that with the service manager. Ask to see how much time the mechanic had into the job, and be shown what was done. Ask to see the mechanic's time card punch for the repair order that was produced for the work needed on your car. You will probably get this as a first explanation: "We put two mechanics on the job to get it done faster for you." In that case, there should be two separate time card punches stuck to the repair order. Ask to see them. If the mechanic gets a 3.0 hour service or repair done in 2.0 to 2.5 hours, this can be acceptable—that is, if everything is done. Most dealerships, and some independent shops, will have a service menu. Compare what was done on your car to what is on the service menu.

Let me explain the flat rate in a different way. A worker in a light bulb factory must inspect 100 light bulbs in 30 minutes without missing any defective bulbs. The worker will get 1 hour of pay. If the worker misses defective light bulbs and they get shipped out to a vendor, then if the bulbs are returned, the worker must re-inspect or repair on their own time, for free. Make sense? In any job where production is involved, there is a delicate balance between quality and quantity. It is important, in this day in age, to get what you pay for. Good customer service is getting harder to find. It's out there, but you have to take the time to find it! If you are unable to accept or understand the flat-rate pay system, you may want to seek a shop that pays their mechanics hourly. However, in a shop like this, it may be more difficult to find and figure out what the shop charged you for a particular labor operation.

The flat-rate pay system is designed to benefit the customer, the business, and the employee, but unfortunately some human beings are unable to control issues with greed in almost any form of employment. A good, honest flat-rate automotive technician who produces between 125% and 135% productivity with no come-backs is acceptable. A mechanic who produces over 135% efficiency is more than likely not performing all the service that he should be. They may have a lot of new parts stored away in their toolbox. A technician with percentages above 135% is likely to have come-backs. Fixing a problem right the first time may not exactly be that mechanic's specialty! Don't feel awkward asking to see your old parts. A good automotive repair shop will gladly show you the old parts they removed and replaced from your car.

I personally worked under the flat-rate pay system for eigh-teen of my twenty-six years of experience as an automotive repair technician. I stayed right around 120% to 130% efficiency. Could I produce more than that? Sure I could, but I also need to sleep at night! It is hard to sleep at night not knowing, if you left something loose, if you know what I am saying. Not to mention that you want your customers to come back to have you work on their car again. I am now currently employed at a shop that pays by the hour and with no flat rate—no flat rate, not as much stress.

For many years I worked alongside with some very talented mechanics who did not abuse the flat-rate pay system. However, I did work alongside a handful of talented mechanics over the years who did abuse the flat-rate pay system. They could not resist greed. This is especially unfortunate when you have a repair shop with six mechanics, five of them honest, and one not. In years past I worked with one guy who preferred to take the oil filter off with his hand—if he couldn't, he would not replace it. He would then take the brand-new oil filter and throw it in the trash!

Needless to say, a guy like that is more than likely not going to check your tire pressures. Remember to remove a valve stem cap on one of your tires and see if it is replaced after you get your car serviced. If it is not replaced, the mechanic likely did not inspect your tire pressures. Most importantly, the service manager should take notice of this kind of behavior and should correct it immediately! If you're shopping around for an auto repair shop, make sure you ask whether the mechanics are paid under the flat-rate pay system. Ask how they arrived at their labor times in their estimates. I want you to fully understand that the flat-rate pay system is not bad in a shop that is well-managed, organized, and has disciplined quality control.

With the many variables that come up with the flat-rate pay system, I would personally recommend you try to find a shop that pays their mechanics hourly or by salary. This way, you will have the best chance to be treated fairly when it comes to your repair bill. You should receive high-quality work every time. Find a mechanic who is personable and enjoys talking to his or her customers. Know who your mechanic is and know your mechanic is working on your car when you bring it in for repairs or service.

In today's world it takes a lot to be a good automotive repair technician. You would not believe what it costs a mechanic to buy a tool box and fill it with tools these days. Through the years, I have heard in certain circles that the general public thinks that automotive dealerships pay for the mechanic's tools, or that the mechanic just plugs a scan tool into the car when the check engine light comes on and it fixes the problem. This is not true; mechanics own or are paying for their tools. Some mechanics may owe more for their tool boxes and tools inside than you may owe on your mortgage!

Yes, it is true that dealerships are required to have certain specialty tools to work on their product. The dealership is required to pay for and owns those special tools. A mechanic who works for a dealership is, however, provided with technical training to keep current with the product. A mechanic who works for an independent repair shop must fend for himself to keep current on technology for all makes and models of automobiles.

The scan tool basically points the mechanic in the right direction, as to what the problem may be with your car. He still has to roll up his sleeves and possibly do a little head scratching to fix the problem. I do not want to forget to mention that today's automotive technician can expect to pay anywhere between $5,000 and $10,000 for a good scan tool. He also has to pay to have the software for the scan tool to be updated annually. When you bring your car in with the check engine light on and they find out what the problem is and fix it in 30 minutes, but charge you 1 hour labor for the diagnosis and repair, I recommend that you do not argue about it. 75% of the time, a repair is not a quick fix!

If you just had your car serviced and you find that the mechanic left a tool behind in your car, please return it—you will make his day and establish a great relationship with your mechanic! I hope that after reading this, you have a better idea about what it takes to run an auto repair shop and what it takes to be an automotive repair technician in today's world. When you find a good mechanic, do not let him go!

Why is this mechanic unable to find a tool he needs,
when he needs it?

If you want to establish a good relationship between your service advisor, your mechanic, and yourself, <u>below is a list of thirty-one things not to do </u>when you bring your car in for service. Yes, these things do actually happen. You cannot make these things up!

1) Don't bring your car in to have us diagnose a drive-ability complaint, with your fuel gauge below empty and the low fuel light on.
2) Don't complain that ever since you had your oil changed, your car vibrates when you apply your brakes.
3) Don't call up to make an appointment and put the service advisor on hold.
4) Don't make your service appointment, then fail to show up for it, come in the following day, say you forgot, and you want it done now.

5) Don't bring your vehicle in for state inspection without giving us your vehicle's registration. Then don't be unavailable at the phone number you provided us, so we can ask you where the registration may be. When you finally call us to see if your car is ready, we ask you where your registration is. You say it is in the glove box. We already looked there and could not find it. The registration was in your pocket the whole time!

6) Don't bring your car in for the shop to diagnose a noise, tell us it is not making the noise today, and then get mad when we are unable to tell you what it is.

7) Don't bring your truck in for a front end alignment and leave your snow plow on, after driving through a manure-filled pasture.

8) Get your vehicle oil undercoated just before your mechanic does some major suspension repair. By comparison, it would be like eating a whole sleeve of Oreo cookies just before going to the dentist to get your teeth cleaned.

9) Don't drop your car off for service that requires wheel removal and then tell us you don't know where your wheel lock key is ... or what a wheel lock key is.

10) Don't ask us to check your spare tire pressure if the trunk is packed with camping gear, fishing tackle, and dirty laundry.

11) Don't put your vehicle's after-market security system in valet mode, so the alarm goes off continually while the vehicle is up in the air on a hoist ... good times.

12) If you are a doctor or a lawyer, don't ask for a professional discount.

13) Don't have the shop diagnose your problem, then tell them you do not have any money to fix your car, then complain about the labor charge for time it took to diagnose your car.

14) Don't bring your snow tires in to be mounted, full of stagnant

water and old leaves—or worse yet, full of water that has frozen solid. Then don't get upset when the tires we dismounted were not put in tire bags. Also, please try to avoid bringing in the wrong-size tires from your other car!

15) Don't smoke three cigarettes with your windows up and make sure your vent position is on recirculation with the heater fan on high speed, just before the mechanic with respiratory issues gets into your car.

16) After your mechanic gets your car fully lifted into the air on the hoist with your engine oil draining into an oil bucket, don't ask if you can get something in your car.

17) Ask for a front end alignment, get the alignment done, then complain that your car still vibrates. Please know the difference between when you need an alignment done and your wheels balanced.

18) Don't leave your dog in the car, so when the unsuspecting mechanic gets into your car your dog barks, jumps on his lap, or licks his ear while he is driving your car into the shop.

19) Don't come in late for your service appointment, on a Friday afternoon at 4:30 pm, to have your new snow tires mounted just before a big snow storm. Then don't have a meltdown because the last set of snow tires in your size were sold at the time you were supposed to show up for your appointment.

20) After you get the call that your car is ready, don't come to pick your car up for a week, and then complain that there is never enough parking.

21) Don't fail to rotate your new tires for 10,000 miles and then state that you don't understand why your tires wore out so quickly!

22) Don't leave your kayaks on the roof rack of your car so the mechanic can lift the car only halfway with the hoist. This is worst when your car needs exhaust work.

23) Have the parts department special order parts for you, and then wait for a month to make an appointment to get the parts replaced when you get the call that your special order has arrived. Or if you do this, at least don't get upset when the parts have been sent back.

24) Don't tell your mechanic to just do whatever the car needs to have done, and then complain about the bill.

25) Don't bring in your own parts to be replaced and have them be the wrong parts for your car, and then ask why it took so long to repair your car!

26) When you go to a new auto repair shop and you have a problem that needs to be diagnosed on your car, tell them what your mechanic thinks is wrong with your car.

27) If the driver's side front door has a little pocket to pull the door shut from the inside don't stuff a dirty Kleenex tissue there, so when your mechanic goes to pull the door shut, he unknowingly buries his fingers in your used Kleenex as he shuts the door. Nice.

28) Don't drive your vehicle in with a foot of snow on the roof, trunk, and hood, and make the mechanic clean the snow off.

29) Don't have your car towed in because it ran out of gas, and then complain that you have to pay the tow bill.

30) Don't bounce a check.

31) If your driver's side front power window only goes down but not up, don't fail to tell us about it ... and don't expect your mechanic to remove the door panel to get the window back up for free!

CHAPTER 11
Maintenance for Your Car

Shown above is an odometer from one of my customers' vehicles.

I would like to start this chapter off by strongly recommending that you go to one repair shop and get to know your mechanic personally. If you like your mechanic's work and recommendations for service work needed, stick with that mechanic. If you just purchased a used car that has fairly low mileage—for example, it has 30,000 miles—I'm going to make recommendations to you that may seem like overkill. When I started working at the Honda dealership in 1985, the way that cars were serviced back then may seem like overkill today. Sparkplugs were being changed at 15,000-mile intervals, as well as transmission fluid and valve adjustments. You do have to keep in mind that the labor rate in 1985 at the Honda dealership was $28 an hour! Guess what? As labor rates increased, what you had to do on your car decreased.

I believe it was Ford that started the no scheduled tune-up for 100,000 miles. This effort was to keep the cost of ownership down to make it more attractive for you to buy their vehicles. Then the vicious cycle started when everybody started buying Fords because it cost so little to service them, as this is what they were told. Many of the automakers followed suit—GM and Chrysler, then later on, other automakers such as Honda and Toyota, with others to follow. With my experience over the years, I have seen a lot of changes in the auto industry. I have seen how servicing a vehicle the right way causes it to last a very long time. I have seen vehicles serviced the wrong way or not at all, with an end result of high repair bills and frequent breakdowns, with the feared and dreaded engine and transmission failures!

Why do you want a car that is going to break down? Don't you want a vehicle that is going to be trouble-free and dependable? If you look in the owner's manual in the maintenance section, it may tell you to service your car under normal or severe conditions. It is my recommendation to you that you follow the maintenance schedule for severe conditions. I want to prepare you because you're going to say to your mechanic, "I read this book and it's telling me that I need to service my car under the severe service conditions schedule in the owner's manual." I guarantee you that your mechanic is going to tell you, "You don't need to service your car under the severe conditions guidelines." Maybe he will say that just to get your business, but it won't help you in the long run, with the cost of ownership of your vehicle. If you service your vehicle the way I recommend and you drive the well-engineered car conservatively, you should get 200,000 to 300,000 miles out of your car.

When I say drive your car conservatively, that means no jack-rabbit starts from traffic lights, no quick or abrupt braking, and you should drive around the potholes, not directly into them! Get the idea? If you buy a well-engineered used car with 30,000 miles or less, with maintenance records, you have the best chance of meeting this goal. You must also keep your car washed to remove road salt, to prevent your car or truck from rusting away from you!

Here's schedule to follow. This very schedule is the one I use on my personal vehicle and my wife's personal vehicle. If you buy the vehicle with 30,000 miles or so on it, I recommend that you replace all the fluids in the vehicle right from the start. Then stick a label somewhere under the hood for each fluid that was replaced, with the date and mileage on it, or keep your service records in your car. If you have a filing system in your home, keep the records there. Keep in mind—I mean a filing system for your service records! Don't throw them in the junk drawer by the fridge. You will not find them when you need them, and you surely will need them in the future! I have had customers call me in the past and ask me if they have had their timing belt replaced yet! I then ask them what they had for lunch a month ago, to get the point across!

Before I get too deep into fluid replacement, I want you to know that I do not particularly care for the terms "flush," "power flush," or "flushing of fluids." Why? When your automatic transmission fluid is replaced with a machine, you need to know that the fluid is "exchanged," not power flushed. Most automatic transmission fluid changing equipment uses the pump pressure from the transmission to evacuate the old fluid. Then the transmission is filled with new fluid with a low-pressure pump in the exchange equipment. Power flushing, in my opinion, is an unnecessary description of service. It is a marketing ploy to lead you to believe you are getting more for your money.

If you change your fluids in your car on a regular basis, you should never have the need to exchange any fluids in the car. The key here is to replace the fluid before it gets too dirty. If you do purchase a vehicle with higher mileage, let's say between 60,000 and 90,000 miles, exchanging the fluids out may be a better idea. However, as far as an automatic transmission goes, you may want to do a series of drains and refills to the automatic transmission until the fluid looks new again. If the filter in the automatic transmission is replaceable, you should replace it if you already have the pan off the transmission.

It may sound like I'm contradicting myself here, but you do want to be careful before you exchange the transmission fluid out with higher mileage on it. Sometimes when a vehicle has higher mileage on it, exchanging the fluid in the transmission may disturb sediment, causing certain critical passages in the automatic transmission to be blocked, thus causing transmission failure. That type of situation would be counterproductive, would it not? I recommend that you change your vehicle's automatic transmission fluid every _2 to 3 years or 30,000 miles,_ whichever comes first. If you tow a camper, a boat, or a trailer on a regular basis, you may want to change your fluid every year or _7,500 to 10,000 miles_. If you have a truck with a snow plow or you work the truck fairly hard, you may want to follow this schedule as well.

I have had great success through the years with reliability in all my vehicles. My successful results can be attributed to two basic facts. _First:_ I have replaced the fluids in all of my vehicles as I repetitively recommend. _Second:_ I drive my vehicles normally. I do not abuse them. I avoid jackrabbit starts when the traffic lights turn green. I avoid holes in the road. I drive defensively, not offensively. I pay attention to all gauges and warning lights. Your results may vary due to your personal driving habits and choice or make of vehicle. If you want your car to last and be reliable, and you are in it for the long haul, I suggest you service your car as I recommend below.

- ☑ *Make sure you always use only fluids recommended by the automotive manufacturer!*
- ☑ Change your engine oil and oil filter every 4,000 to 5,000 miles with synthetic motor oil.
- ☑ A Change of power steering fluid should be done every 15,000 miles.
- ☑ Manual transmission oil should be replaced every 15,000 to 25,000 miles.
- ☑ Brake fluid should be replaced every two years or 24,000 miles, whichever comes first.
- ☑ Antifreeze should be replaced every two years or 30,000 miles, whichever comes first, and should <u>always</u> be mixed with distilled water. You may want to replace the thermostat at this interval as well. Proper PH is important so that it does not get too acidic. I personally ignore what long-life antifreeze manufactures say for replacement intervals.
- ☑ Your cabin air filter should be replaced 15,000 miles, or more frequently under dusty conditions.
- ☑ Your engine air filter should be inspected at every oil change and replaced before it gets too dirty. Always replace your air filter with a high-quality air filter, as keeping dirt from entering your engine is crucial to engine longevity. The air cleaner case and cover must be free of cracks. The cover must fit securely. This is also a good time to have your mass air flow sensor cleaned.
- ☑ You should change your differential fluids and transfer case fluids at least every 20,000 to 30,000 miles, or more frequently under severe working or wet conditions.

☑ Change your engine oil and filter every 3,000 to 5,000 miles with synthetic oil. Check all fluid levels at the midpoint of 1,500 to 2,500 miles.

☑ Check all the tire pressures weekly with a tire pressure gauge, or at least walk around the vehicle before you drive to see if any of the tires are noticeably soft. If a tire is low on air, adjust the tire pressure as needed. Bring it to your mechanic and have the tire checked for a leak. Have the tire repaired, if it can be safely repaired. Check your spare tire pressure, especially if you are going on a trip. Most fatal accidents are caused by poor tires or low tire pressures. You should always adjust your tire pressures according to the manufacturer's label located on the inside edge of the driver's door or door jamb. Never inflate the tire to the maximum rating on the side of the tire.

☑ If the vehicle has adjustable valves, they should be adjusted every 30,000 to 40,000 miles.

☑ If you hear a new noise or rattle in your car, don't just turn up your radio—have it checked out!

☑ Rotate and balance the wheels every 5,000 miles of driving. Ask the mechanic to take a peek at your brakes at this point in time. Make sure no wheels are dragging due to stuck brake pads.

☑ Get your car to a car wash in the winter months. Keep road salt off the car!

☑ Have your alignment checked and adjusted annually or every 12,000 to 15,000 miles, especially if you live in an area prone to frost heaves and potholes. Get the alignment done after the bumpy season is over. Always have an alignment done when you replace your tires.

☑ Keep the inside of your car clean. This will make a difference, if and when you want to trade it in or sell it.

☑ Have your car checked for recalls. Yours may have gotten lost in the mail or thrown away mistakenly for junk mail.

☑ External drive belts need to be replaced at the first signs of cracking.

☑ Timing belts (if equipped) need to be replaced per the owner's manual or service manual's recommendations.

☑ Keep all service records and receipts. Place labels under your engine's hood, stating what fluid or filter was replaced and when.

Most people who have cabin air filters don't know they have one, or don't know that it needs to be replaced. This customer was unknowingly breathing the air that passed through the cabin filter into their car on the left. Filter on right is the new one that replaced it. After the filter was replaced, the customer's allergies cleared up. Imagine that.

In any case, follow the maintenance schedule in your owner's manual for severe conditions. Simply put, most components that may fail in your vehicle are damaged due to excessive heat. As the fluid gets older and dirtier, its ability to remove heat is greatly diminished. This is why it is important to replace the fluid in question before it gets too dirty. Please understand that condensation (moisture) in fluids may require you to exchange them before you hit mileage replacement requirements. If you follow these recommendations, combined with good driving habits, a well-engineered vehicle could quite possibly never have component failure.

I know that at some point, my vehicle service recommendations will come up in conversation. It may be that your Uncle Bill's friend used to be a mechanic fifteen years ago. He says, "You don't have to change your fluids until they turn black!" Well, the next time you are driving down the road and you see someone broken down with their engine hood open, staring at it hopelessly, they probably listened to your Uncle Bill's friend.

The Brakes

The most important part of your brake system, in most cases, is the most neglected: the brake fluid. This fluid should be replaced every two years, as it attracts moisture. Most automotive manufacturers do not have a replacement interval for this fluid, which is kind of scary.

Look at this brake rotor that needs to be replaced.

Brake pads should be inspected annually for freedom of

movement. If the brake pads do not move freely in the brackets, as they are designed to, this can cause your brakes to overheat. This is especially not good if your brake fluid has a high content of moisture in it. When the brake pads are stuck in the brackets, it is like driving around with your foot on the brake pedal. Needless to say, this does not help your fuel mileage at all! When the brake fluid has too much moisture, it will boil if overheated. When this happens, it causes the brake fluid to aerate with tiny bubbles, causing brake pedal to fade and become spongy, putting you in a dangerous situation. Servicing your brakes annually and replacing the brake fluid on a regular schedule will provide you with peace of mind for the most important system in your vehicle—the system that allows you to stop!

If your mechanic tells you that one of your brake calipers has a seized caliper pin and needs to be serviced, I suggest that you spend the extra money and replace the caliper. Here is why. Each caliper usually has two pins that are lubricated with special brake grease, and each is sealed with a little rubber boot. When these boots fail, they allow moisture in. The caliper can be freed, but when the old boot is reused, it is only a temporary fix as it allows moisture in and seizes the pin once again. When this happens, it usually ruins the new brake parts you replaced six months ago. Why not just replace the failed boots? The boots that seal the caliper pins are not usually available, and it is better in the long run to replace the caliper and be done with it. Another problem can develop when caliper pins are lubricated with too much or the wrong type of grease. This can cause the pins to actually not move as they were designed to do, because they are overwhelmed with grease. Some caliper pins have a little rubber tip installed on them, and if you use a petroleum-based grease, it can cause the rubber tip to swell and not move within the cavity it was designed to move within.

It is also important to make sure that your brake fluid reservoir is not overfilled. When the brake fluid reservoir is overfilled, the brake fluid can expand as it gets warmer. It has nowhere to go, building up pressure in the hydraulic system, and can act as if your foot is resting on the brake pedal. This usually happens when you have had brake pads replaced. A mechanic squeezes the caliper in, to accept the new brake pads, thus pushing brake fluid back into the reservoir, causing it to be overfilled. A good mechanic will take the time to loosen the brake bleeder on the caliper and connect an appropriate hose to it; then he squeezes the caliper in and collects the old brake fluid into an appropriate container. You should never push brake fluid back into the brake fluid reservoir, especially with vehicles that have ABS systems. The hydraulic brake system is designed to have the fluid travel in the direction it was designed to flow.

If you bring your vehicle for service and they say they will check all fluids and top them off if they are low, they may not be doing you any favors. Most brake fluid reservoirs have a minimum level and a maximum level, and the level serves as a wear indicator. When your brake pads get low, the fluid is displaced into the caliper, lowering the fluid in the brake fluid reservoir. When the brake fluid level gets low enough because of excessive brake pad wear, the brake warning lamp should illuminate on the dash. Usually it is the same light that will come on when you leave your parking brake on. If you bring your car in for service, and they tell you a certain fluid was low, you need to ask the question, "Why is the fluid low, and where did the fluid go?"

As I mentioned before, about brake pads sticking in the brackets, you can alleviate this problem by having your brakes disassembled and serviced annually with good synthetic brake grease. Why do brake pads stick in their brackets? What happens here is that rust forms between the brake pad and the bracket, leaving no clearance for the brake pads to move freely, as they were designed to. The situation is more prevalent in the northeast or parts of the country or world where the vehicle is exposed to winter months of driving. Can this be costly? Not so much. It should take your mechanic only about an hour to perform the labor to do this per axle. The brake pad can be slightly modified with a file or other device to add more clearance where it is needed for the brake pad to move freely. When material is removed from the brake pad movement point, it will take more time for rust to form in this clearance area to cause the brake pad to bind in the bracket. If you notice that your brake pedal feels low or spongy, this may indicate to you that your brake pads are stuck in the brackets and need to be serviced. However, brake pads cannot always be serviced if they have to be hammered out of the brackets. There may be a chance that the brake pads will crumble. At this point in time, you may have to have your brake pads replaced. Please know this: When a brake pad is 50% worn, the second half of a brake pad's life wears out much more quickly than the first 50%, mostly due to the fact the brake pad's ability to absorb and dissipate heat is greatly diminished.

If your brake pads crumble and fall apart, you will want to replace the brake rotors at the same time. More than likely if the brake pads crumble and fall apart it's because they have been overheated, and the brake rotors have been overheated, as well. In this case, you should always replace the brake rotors with the pads and brake pads with rotors. When possible always go with OEM (original equipment manufacturer) quality brake parts.

If you want to save a little bit of money and go with after-market brake parts, be careful with that decision, because this can be known as bending over a dollar to pick up a dime! Sure, after-market brakes may be fine at first, but you may find as time goes by that you end up with a brake vibration or noisy brakes. Every time you feel that brake vibration or hear that brake noise, you will think about the $25 that you saved by buying after-market brake parts!

You may not have a problem buying after-market brake pads or other after-market brake parts. Just make sure that if you do make the choice to buy after-market brake parts, you do not go with the cheapest parts available. It's your choice; it's your life!

The Hand Brake or Parking Brake

Many cars that have an automatic transmission do not get regular usage of the parking brake or hand brake. More times than not, what happens a friend borrows your car and when they park the car and pull up on the parking brake (that you never use), it will not release. Bummer! If your car is driven in this condition, you might notice smoke pouring out of the rear brakes when your friend pulls back into the driveway. In this case, you will likely have to replace your rear brakes and emergency brake cables, which can be quite costly. It is important to use your parking brake on a regular basis, when you park your car, regardless of whether you have an automatic or standard transmission. It will then work when you need it to. The hand brake is not designed to stop the vehicle. It is designed only to hold the vehicle secure in a parked position. A good mechanic will check the parking brake for proper function during a state inspection and should inform you if the parking brake needs to be adjusted. If you plan on storing your vehicle for a long period of time, you should not set your parking brake, if your car is equipped with brake shoes. I have seen brake linings stick to the drum with surface rust. The brake shoes had to be replaced. To assure that the vehicle will not move, you can purchase some wheel chocks to place under the wheels.

Tires

The most important thing between you and the road is your tires. I don't know if you remember or not, but Michelin had the best commercial ever, with a baby sitting in the middle of the tire—that pretty much says it all. When the time comes to replace your tires, take into consideration that the tires are just that: the most important thing between you and the road! Most people, if they are on a budget, will purchase the cheapest tires they can. Sometimes you can luck out and get a set of cheap tires that are actually round! Another common problem with cheap tires is that sometimes the steel belt is not centered perfectly within the tire. This can cause the vehicle to pull to the left or right. Oh sure, you could rotate the tires to the rear and the pulling may go away. However, the pulling will return when you rotate the tires back to the front. The only way to correct this permanently is to replace the defective tire.

It can be a bit confusing when it comes time to buy tires. I usually do not go for the most expensive tires or the cheapest tires. I try to purchase tires that are priced in the middle of the road. It's the best chance of getting a decent quality tire at an affordable price. If you can afford them, Michelin tires are the best you can get! I have mounted brand-new Michelin tires that did not take any weight to balance them. Most tires, when balanced on a machine, need wheel weights pounded onto the rim in specific locations. You get what you pay for when it comes to tires, and also you can also pay for what you get with tires!

On the side of the tire you will find various numbers, such as the tire size—for example, P 235/70/16. This is the number that you are to write down to get prices on tires. You can order tires over the internet and get them shipped to you; however, the money that you saved disappears after paying for shipping the tires. If you want your tires to last a long time, there are tread wear numbers on the side of the tires, for example let's say the tread wear is 520. As far as tread wear numbers go, the higher the number the better—or the longer the tire will last. Low tread wear numbers will wear out very quickly. You will not be happy with the tire's lifespan. If you are looking at a tire with a tread wear rating of 520 and a temperature and traction rating of A, this would be an excellent tire to purchase.

Keep in mind that you need to rotate your tires and check the tire pressures regularly, to get maximum life expectancy from your tires.

You must understand that the tread wear grade is a comparative rating, based on the tread wear rating of the tire when tested under controlled conditions, on a specified government test course. In actuality, the tread wear number can offer you only an approximate lifespan, as road conditions and driver habits will greatly affect tire wear and the lifespan of the tires. Remember, as a tire gets lower on tread, the tire's ability to pump water from the center of the tire to the outside is greatly diminished. Hydroplaning can then be a greater possibility.

Traction grades, from the highest to the lowest, are AA,* A, B, and C. Those grades represent the tire's ability to stop on wet pavement, as measured under controlled conditions, on specified test surfaces of asphalt and concrete. A tire marked C may have poor traction performance. Traction grades assigned to most tires are based on straight-ahead braking traction tests. They do not include acceleration, cornering, hydroplaning, or peak traction characteristics.

Temperature grades, from highest to lowest, are A, B, and C. They represent the tire's resistance to heat generation and its ability to dissipate heat, when tested under controlled conditions, on a specified indoor laboratory test wheel. This, of course, means that the tire is to be properly inflated and not overloaded. Never mix different tire sizes. Do not ever mix symmetrical tires with directional tires, as this can cause handling issues—you do not want to find out about the hard way!

In Europe, a tire that is six years old is considered a bad tire and must be discarded, as they can be dry rotted. There are a lot of cars on the road in the US that have tires that are over six years old. I personally believe it is a good idea to discard a tire after a certain amount of time. Whether or not there will be a time guide reference like this in the US is uncertain, but I believe there should be.

I personally recommend that you do not purchase directional tires, as you cannot easily rotate the tires left to right. The only way to do this with a directional tire is to dismount them, flip them over, and remount and balance them. At this point, the tires would not be worth the labor to do so. I recommend that you stay with symmetrical tires. Asymmetrical tires are okay as you can rotate them side to side without dismounting the tires. It seems that everyone drives differently. Every car seems to wear tires a little differently. The salesperson at the tire store needs to ask you the proper questions, so you can receive the maximum benefit from the tires. You want the longest lifespan possible. With proper tire inflation and scheduled tire rotation, you can get it! Be methodical in your search for tires. Don't let the tire store try to sell you tires that they need to move. Do your homework, as your tires are truly the only thing between you and the road!

Spare Tire

Please take notice of the writing on the side of your temporary spare tire. It says "Temporary spare tire Max speed 40 mph!" The tire is designed to get you home or to the shop to get your REAL tire fixed! I have seen cars pass me on the highway with these tires on. I could not believe it! It is very dangerous to do that, not to mention that most of these space-saver tires are almost never inflated to the proper tire pressure. It makes the situation even more dangerous!

I strongly recommend that you familiarize yourself with your car's spare tire, tools, and jack and how to use them. If you do not feel comfortable doing this yourself, you need to have somebody who knows how to change a tire show you how to do it. Of course, if you are handicapped, I recommend you become a AAA member, and with just a phone call, someone will come to change your flat for you. Your owner's manual has detailed instructions about changing a flat tire as well. Always change your tire on a flat level surface!

Always! Never change a tire on a busy highway or street.

Most trucks or mini vans, and some sport utility vehicles, carry the spare tire underneath; the tire is held up tight to the bottom of the vehicle with a winch and cable. These spare tire winches should be operated from time to time to verify that they work and the cable is not rusted or frayed. When you get a flat and need to lower your spare tire and it has never been lowered, guess what? The winch will be seized—good times! Again, you should take the time to know where your spare tire tools and jack are, and how to use them, before you get a flat. Take a nice weekend day and change your own tire by following the instructions in your owner's manual.

I feel that I need to share this story with you. A guy brought his truck into have his exhaust repaired at our shop. Approximately six months later, he came back to our shop and confronted the mechanic who replaced the exhaust on his truck. He said to him, "I got a flat tire and I went to lower my spare tire down, and it was gone! What did you do with my spare tire? It was there before you replaced my exhaust!" The mechanic explained that he did not have to lower his spare tire to replace his exhaust. He had no need for his spare tire. *The mechanic got underneath his truck and could clearly see that the cable had frayed and then broken!* Most likely when he was driving down the road, when he hit a bump, the tire fell off. You can see exactly how important it is that this cable or chain is inspected, to make sure it is safe and not frayed. It would make a bad day for someone who is traveling behind you at highway speeds, to have your spare tire come flying through their windshield!

Snow Tires

Are you excited? You just purchased four brand-new snow tires. You are ready for whatever winter has to throw your way. Make sure that you put your snow tires on as late in the season as possible, as your new snow tires will wear out quickly if driven on dry pavement. If you can get two winters' worth of driving out of your snow tires, you are doing well. You may not realize this, but when a snow tire becomes half worn it is no longer a snow tire, but it is now basically an all-season tire. When your snow tire is brand-new it may measure 12/32nds of an inch, but halfway worn it measures 6/32nds and should be considered an all-season tire. Many people have their snow tires taken off their car and they are basically considered all-season tires. Before you have your snow tires taken off in the spring, you should ask your mechanic to measure the tread depth, or just do a visual inspection. Ask your mechanic if the tires will be good in the snow next year.

If your mechanic tells you the tires will not be good in the snow next year, you may want to leave the old snow tires on through the summer and get new snow tires in the fall. This way you can save your summer tires for the following spring, when you take off your new snow tires. Basically, if you do this, you can make your summer tires last longer! You may not be able to do this if you have studded tires, as some states require that you remove studded tires by a certain time in the spring. Also, if your snow tires have a lot of road noise when driving, you probably cannot wait to get them off your car! Most people will put up with the noisy tires to save some money.

If you need the best traction possible, studded snow tires are your best bet. You must always use four studded snow tires. If you have a front-wheel drive vehicle and you think you can just place two studded snow tires on the front of your car, think again. You need to have four tires of equal traction. This keeps the rear end of your vehicle on the road in slippery conditions.

Nitrogen-filled Tires

You may have driven past a tire store at some point and seen a green strobe light flashing indicating that tires are being filled with nitrogen. I do not personally see anyone benefiting from filling their tires with nitrogen instead of regular compressed air. They do, however, give you a pretty green valve stem cap when you pay to have your tires filled with nitrogen! Apparently, I have learned the molecules in nitrogen are fat, as opposed to plain old oxygen. The chubby nitrogen molecules are less apt to pass through the porous tire surface. The skinny oxygen molecules are more apt to pass through the porous surface, causing you to have to check your tire pressures more often. *Sure.* Less than 60% of the population will check their tire pressures on a regular basis. If the tire store you are thinking of purchasing tires from offers to fill your tires with nitrogen for free, by all means go for it! As far as paying for it out of pocket, I would personally join the 40% that check their tire pressures on a regular basis. Save your money to buy a tire pressure gauge. There is no real proven benefit to filling your tires with nitrogen for a passenger vehicle. The only vehicles that may benefit from nitrogen filled tires would be for automotive racing. Stable tire temperatures and pressures can be can be crucial for maximum tire wear on asphalt in automotive racing.

The Suspension

You should pay attention to any new noises when driving over bumps. Also, you should take notice of differences in handling characteristics when you are on the road. As you drive your car, no one will know the car like you do; you will know when something does not feel right. You should have your car looked at if something does not feel right with it, even if it just passed state inspection the month before!

The Battery and Charging System

When I service a vehicle, I always check and test the battery. Your battery can be trusted for about four to five years. A battery that tests good one day could fail the following day, if exposed to excessive heat or cold. Also, a battery that may test good could still be weak. A weak battery will cause your starter to work harder, because the battery does not have the cranking amperage that it once had. Your alternator will also have to work harder to try to replenish or keep the battery charged fully. A weak battery can cause premature failure of your starter, alternator, and other electrical components in your car. If your battery is four to five years old, I recommend that it be replaced to provide you with maximum reliability. Make sure you replace your battery with a good-quality replacement battery. Don't buy the cheapest one on the shelf!

Corroded battery terminals or battery posts can be cleaned, but this condition will return. A battery can test okay, but if the battery posts have corrosion, the battery should be replaced. Also, the charging system needs to be checked to make sure that the alternator is not overcharging, causing the acid to boil out of the battery via the battery terminal posts. If you plan on installing a large amp to boost your stereo system, make sure your alternator can handle it. You may "cook it," if your alternator is unable to produce the amperage to power it effectively. This principle can also apply to power inverters.

Make sure your mechanic uses a memory saver when replacing your battery. A memory saver is like a temporary life support, while replacing your battery. Without using a memory saver, in today's cars you will erase the memory. On certain models you may have to perform a relearn procedure. Most European vehicles have to go to the dealership to have this procedure performed, if a memory saver is not used. Never ever create a spark or flame near a battery—it can explode!

Protecting Your Paint

At least twice a year, try to use a high-quality wax on your vehicle to protect the paint. If you have a bird leave a deposit on your car, hose it off as soon as you can. This nasty stuff can burn and bake into your paint, causing permanent damage. After you wax your car and it rains on your car, you will notice that the water beads up nicely and rolls off, but not all of it does. When the sky clears and the sun comes out, these remaining beads of water are heated by the sun, acting like little magnifying glasses. They can burn little water spot circles into your paint. This can also cause permanent damage. Get yourself a drying chamois; you can purchase them at almost any parts store or department store.

Here's a quick note about black vehicles. If you want a black car and have never owned one, you should be aware that it takes a lot of work to keep them looking nice. Have a black car if you must, but make sure if you do that you stock up on elbow grease, because you are going to need it!

Never allow brake fluid to get on your paint for any reason! If this does happen, wipe it off immediately or hose it off with water. Brake fluid will remove paint almost instantly if you do not act quickly! Make sure that when you notice paint chips, you cover them up with touch-up paint, before the rust starts. You can usually get touch-up paint from any parts store. Consult your owner's manual to find the paint code for your car. You may have to visit the dealer for the maker of your car to get the proper paint to match your car, if touch-up paint is not available in local stores.

Follow what I have recommended in this chapter for maintaining your car, and you should have a car that will last you a long time. Trouble-free, reliable transportation is what you are aiming for. I also hope that the information about what it takes to be an automotive technician in this day in age may help you better understand what goes on after you hand your service advisor the keys to your car.

CHAPTER 12

When to Trade, Sell, or Just Say Goodbye to Your Old Car

When is it time? When do you get rid of your old car? Sooner or later, that ol' reliable car is going to let you down at the worst possible time. Perhaps it will be raining out and you are halfway home from grocery shopping with the kids. Then the fuel pump decides that it no longer wants to pump fuel for you! When a car gets to be about ten years old, things can start to go wrong without warning. Some cars have expensive things go wrong much sooner than the ten-year mark. Sure, you can keep your car for fifteen years or so, but you will need to keep investing money into maintaining it to make that happen. You might ask yourself, "Is it worth it?" What will be next? The engine, or the transmission?

Nothing lasts forever, but with the help of this book, I would like you to have your vehicle last as long as possible, while staying dependable. You want to take a road trip or go on a vacation, but the old car has been making some new noises lately, even after you just had the car serviced before the trip. Your mechanic tells you that you are all set to go, but somehow your gut feeling tells you that you should not trust this car on a long trip! You cannot really blame your mechanic, either, if something fails in an older vehicle. Of course, if your mechanic has a crystal ball he can gaze into, that may make you rest assured that your car will not break down! If you find yourself renting a new car so you can go on vacation safely, it is probably time to get a newer car.

Perhaps you have had a certain car since it was new, or you purchased one with low miles. This car has never let you down and has been a great car over the years. Maybe it has plagued you with repair bill after repair bill, and you just want to rid yourself of the car once and for all! Realize that if your car is at this point, you probably will not get much money for it, and you should not expect to. If you have driven the wheels off it and you don't owe anything on the car, it is more than likely ready to go to the salvage yard. You might get $200 for it, possibly a little more if you can drive it there.

I am cornered at least three times a year with this question: "Hey, Joe—if I invest $500 into my car, do you think I can get another year out of it?" I usually reply, "I left my crystal ball at home today, so I won't be able to predict the future for you at this point in time." When a car gets to be over ten years old, anything can happen.

We are doing a little role reversal here. You now are the previous owner, whom I had written about in chapter two. Are you willing to disclose everything that you know about your old car? You should be totally honest about the car. Obviously, if it is ready for the salvage yard, you won't have to hide a thing about the car anyway. It may, however, have some parts that may be reusable to someone else.

A friend of mine had a Jeep that would not pass a safety inspection, due to frame rust. He decided not to bring it to the salvage yard; instead he slowly disassembled the Jeep and sold the useable parts on eBay. The salvage yard would give him only $200 for it, fully intact. After he sold everything off it he could, he made $1,200. Not bad for his time and some elbow grease. He later hauled what was left of the Jeep to the salvage yard and got an additional $50 in his pocket. He took the $1,250 and used it as a down payment toward a new set of wheels. If you do not mind the hassle and have some extra time, you could do this yourself. Or you could list the whole car on eBay or Craigslist, as-is, for sale for parts.

If you need to trade in your car, it may be that your vehicle needs have changed, Your family is getting larger and you are running out of room. Or perhaps you want a new car because you're bored with your old car. Just keep in mind that if you do decide to trade your vehicle, you will get the least amount of money for your old car from a dealership. If you trade your car in and it is worth reselling, the dealership will put it on their lot for a retail price. If it is not worth cleaning the car and doing what it needs to pass safety inspection, the dealership will likely send the car to an auction and get what they can for it. The dealer will get more money for it than they gave you to trade it in. That is how they pay the bills to keep their lights on.

The dealership will make money from your trade, and they will make money from selling you a car, period. Car prices, as you know, are placed into three basic categories: retail price, is the highest; private sale is in the middle; and trade-in value will be the lowest. You may bring your car in to a dealership with the intention to trade it in. You have looked online at Kelley Blue Book for the trade-in value of your car. Let's say your car's trade-in value is $3,500, but the salesperson states that they can only give you $500 for your car, because their retail prices are so low on their inventory, or they will tell you they can only give you cash value. Cash value is what they might expect to bring in from auction for your car. At this point, the game will start when you have to basically haggle and talk your way as close as you can to get that trade in value you found on line. If you are unable to get close enough to what you want to get for trade in value you may want to sell your car private sale. An experienced salesperson is ready for you, and has heard every angle from a potential buyer you can imagine. Always keep the ball in your court. Always! Do not let your emotions be taken over by a shiny new or used car. There are thousands of cars to choose from; be patient, and don't be taken advantage of.

Over the past twenty-five years, I have seen customers sink insane amounts of money into their cars, even when they weren't worth sinking one dime into. I have in the past written out huge estimates and strongly recommended that the service advisor *advise* the customer not to invest money into their car if it was not worth it. Guess what? They invest the money into the car foolishly, and six months later something else fails, such as a fuel tank, or several brake lines start leaking due to rust. It is almost always a costly endeavor. In most cases you are caught off-guard and are not financially prepared for it.

The primary reason for investing money into a car is emotional attachment. The car is not just a car to them. Sometimes people get too sentimentally attached to a car. They may have even given the car a name such as Sally or Bob. It has become a part of the family over the years. This can be a sad situation for somebody, especially when they have done all of the services to their car as they were instructed to do. They do not pay attention or try to stop the rust that has been eating away at the vehicle over the years. In some cases you can repair structural rust to buy you some time—that is, if you have something you can weld to ... you see, it is not possible to weld new steel to rust. Structural rust is a serious thing, and it is usually the final nail in the coffin for your car. If you were to get into a serious car accident with a car with structural rust, the crumple zones that your car was engineered with would be greatly affected. You see, these crumple zones are unable to absorb energy in a collision as they were designed to do when the car was new. Here you have a mechanically sound vehicle, but the shell of it is composting back into the earth due to rust! Or you have a vehicle that has a good body and frame, but the engine and transmission are no good! Sometimes with structural rust it is not what you see … it is what you do not see that can hurt you!

As I am writing this book, I am working on a 1989 Honda Civic. The customer has been meticulous over the years in the care of her vehicle. She has kept excellent records, giving us a hand-typed record of what has been done to her car over the past twenty years. Today I have to give her some bad news … the vehicle is rusting away. The vehicle not only is not worth investing money into, but if she were to get into an accident, she could get seriously hurt, mostly because the vehicle's crumple zones are greatly weakened due to structural rust, and it is so old that it does not have airbags. Several years ago she had extensive body work done to her Honda Civic. If I had known at the time that she was about to invest over $2,000 into a car that was worth about $500 or less at the time, I would have advised her to invest that money into buying a new or used car.

She basically drove the car for an additional two years, for over $2,000, and the car is now basically worth $200 to her, from the salvage yard.

It may seem that every time you bring your car in for service the bills get bigger and bigger. Check to see what Blue Book value is on your car. If your car is twelve years old with 200,000 miles on it, and it is worth only $500, then you sink $1,200 into your car and think that your car is worth $1,700, think again. If you sink $1,200 into a car that is worth $500, you still have a car that is worth $500, or less.

Usually people get off to a great start just after they buy a car. The car gets washed and vacuumed on a regular basis. Services are done and service records are kept. But as time goes by, the car loses its appeal, and the owner kind of slacks off the maintenance programs and caring for the vehicle. Next thing you know, they have a

$1,500 repair bill sitting in front of them. Here in the northeastern part of the country, the rust will eventually take over and consume your vehicle right before your eyes! Sadly, this is the time to put your old car out to pasture and say goodbye.

You may say to yourself, "Doing these repairs on my old car is better than a car payment!" But is it? In some cases, yes; if you are out of a job and that old car is all you have for transportation, you may have no choice but to try to hold on to your car for a while, until things get better for you financially. If you do make this choice, know up front what you may be getting yourself into. Money that you invest in this car could be a good down payment on a new or used car that may be more dependable than the one you are in right now. Remember that what you decide to invest in your old car, you should not expect to get a return for it in the future.

Preparing Your Car for Sale or Trade

Maybe your old car is not exactly ready for the bone yard, but you just want a newer car to drive since you are getting bored with your old car.

What is the first thing you need to do before you trade or sell your old car? You need to clean the car, obviously, and you need to clean the car well! This includes removing the *hardened McDonald's french fries* from under the seats of your car. If you are a smoker and you have smoked in your car through the years, good luck getting the smell out! If your car is in decent shape, but it smells like cigarette smoke you, are more than likely going to have to find somebody else who smokes cigarettes to buy your car.

If you sell your car to someone who does not smoke, and you yourself smoke cigarettes and you try to cover up the smell, it is more than likely that the smell will come back soon. You will have a very unhappy camper, probably giving you a very unhappy phone call!

You may have to hire a professional cleaner to clean the inside of your car, if that's the case. Even if they get the smell out, it is quite possible that the smell will return in a short amount of time. One thing you can try is to purchase the biggest can of coffee you can find, open up the can, and set it in the car with the windows up for at least twenty-four hours. This can do a great job of absorbing foul odors. It's worth a shot. Give it a try—I learned this trick when I worked for a professional cleaning company.

If you own dogs and they ride with you on a regular basis, you will probably have a hard time selling it to someone who may have allergies.

While at work, one of my co-worker friends, named Eric, asked me to go outside. A woman had brought her car in to see what he could give her for a trade-in toward another used car. At the time I had another friend looking for a used car. Eric thought it would be a good time to show me this woman's car, while she was standing outside of it. I walked up to the car and she said to me, "Eric tells me that you are looking for a good used car—so what do you think?"

I was struggling to come up with a response; knowing the practical joker Eric was, I almost responded with a laugh, but somehow I kept it together without making eye contact with Eric. The inside of the car had a striking resemblance to a full dumpster! No way was this car anywhere near what I was looking for. I politely told her it was not what I was looking for. Later on that day Eric explained to me the reason he put me on the spot like that. He told me it is unbelievable the horrible condition that people bring their cars in to potentially trade or put on consignment. He wanted me to see firsthand what he was talking about.

It is a good idea to gather all of your service records from your old car, and stick them in a folder, nice and neat, if you can. If you have not been exactly neat about organizing your service records over the years, you may want to ask your repair shop if they can print out your service history. Put the records in a folder and have them ready to view on the front seat for a potential buyer to look at. This is one of the most impressive things you can do, to help sell your car more effectively. It is like having good references or a good résumé when going for a job interview.

Again, as I have mentioned previously in this book, one of the first things you need to look for when buying or looking for a good used car is complete service records. Get your service records together, clean the car, and put that for sale sign in the window!

In this day and age, as sophisticated as vehicles are, we need all the help we can get to find a good, safe, dependable car. Never forget what the previous owner may have exposed the car to. Do not be disappointed if you overlook a problem with a car in your search, such as a little poor bodywork. Over the years even I have overlooked a few things myself when checking out a used car. Remember, a used car will never be perfect it's not always what you see it's what you don't see that matters. If you are methodical in your search, and do your homework, you will find a good dependable used car. Who knows— as sophisticated as cars are getting today, maybe one day that car *will* talk to you and tell you how the previous owner treated it! I wish you luck in your search for a good used vehicle.

Used Car Quick Checklist

1) Shop for a vehicle that suits your needs and not somebody else's. Do you need a truck, car, or minivan? Make sure you surf the web for: 1) Reliability reports for the vehicle you are interested in. Go to Edmunds.com, and/or Kelley blue book.com 2) Cost of ownership 3) Resale value for the vehicle you have in mind.

2) If you are serious about purchasing a vehicle, have a CARFAX done. Do your visual inspection, as mentioned in Chapter 5, noticing collision work.

3) Starting the car for the first time? **Look!** Do you see excessive

blue or white smoke from the tailpipe? **Listen** for excessive noise when first starting the car.

4) Do a walk around the car. Look at it closely for poor or obvious body work.

5) Road testing? Note pulling to left or right while driving. Note vibrations at highway speeds. Note vibrations while applying the brakes. Look in the rearview mirror, under heavy acceleration, for blue or white smoke. Note any transmission slippage in a standard or automatic transmission.

6) Pay attention to the engine temp gauge. It should stay just below halfway. Let the engine idle after the road test long enough until the engine's cooling fan cycles. When the fan cycles, the gauge should still be below the halfway point.

7) Keep your emotions in control! You may be able to afford the monthly payment, but do not lose sight of what it will cost you to register, insure, and maintain the car. In other words, stay within your means.

8) Ask about extended warranties. Careful—the cost of the warranty will depend on the vehicle's reliability report!

9) Ask if your mechanic can look at the car on a hoist, *if you are really considering purchasing the car.*

10) Ask if any or all service records are available. Can the original owner be contacted?

11) Keep the ball in your court at all times! Get the best deal at month's end.

12) If you are trading your old car, get what it is worth, or sell it on your own. Make sure you find out what trade in value is for the vehicle you are thinking of buying. Also find out what the retail price is for the vehicle you are buying. Try to purchase the vehicle between retail and trade in value.

13) Have fun! Drive as many vehicles as possible to find the car

that best suits your needs.

14) If you purchase a used car from a dealership, ask the length of their return period, if a problem arises with the car that is too costly to fix.

15) Don't forget to access the internet to find out just about anything good or bad about the car you are considering buying.

16) Ask somebody who owns the kind of car or truck you are interested in buying if they like it.

About the Author

Ever since I was a kid, I loved taking things apart and trying to figure out how they worked—a radio, a fan, a lawnmower, etc. As I got a little older I developed a strong interest in the operation of the internal combustion engine. I was fascinated by the way it ran. I understood completely and easily how the engine would run, and when the engine would not run, I had to know why. I believe that I was around twelve years old or so when I would go down to the town dump and find old thrown-away lawnmowers and resurrect them to usable condition and sell them to make money for the summer. The best time to sell them was when my mom had yard sales. She had at least one yard sale a year. My mom loved to talk to people, and that was more than likely one of the reasons why she had yard sales—to talk to people. When she ran out of things to sell, she would actually go to yard sales to pick up more items to sell at her yard sales!

I can remember my mom buying a new lawnmower. I may have mowed the lawn twice with it and I had to take the whole thing apart—not because there was something wrong with it; I just got a sudden urge to take it apart and put it back together. To do that and have it actually run again was my goal. It would have been much better not to have my mom walk into the garage to see her son with her brand-new lawnmower torn apart completely. I will never forget the look on her face. Her eyes got real big and I thought I was really in for it. She said, "That lawnmower is going to run again— isn't it, Joseph?" I replied, "Of course it will, Mom; of course it will." After that confrontation I could not help but be a little anxious. I had to make sure that it did go back together correctly.

My older brother David was not mechanically inclined at all. As a matter of fact, I don't think I ever saw him change the oil in his motorcycles. The only time his bikes got any type of attention was when I worked on them. If I did not keep his motorcycle running well, he would take mine and beat the crap out of it! So after the first time he did that, I took the keys out of the bike and hid them. The second time he did it, he figured out how to hotwire my bike to yet again beat the crap out of it! I realized early on that I simply had to keep his bike running well, or else my motorcycle would die an agonizing death!

By the time I was seventeen years old I had bought, ridden, and sold lots of mini bikes and motorcycles. I really wish I had them still, because most of them today would be worth some good money. I had just received my driver's license and was ready for my first car. My mom would let me take the 1977 Plymouth Valiant to the dump or the store, and that was about it. There was no way that I could even think about trying to pick up girls in that car anyway, so I did not get too upset about it. It was a butt-ugly cream color in its slant six-cylinder motor, with its rhythmic ticking valve train. I did not stand a chance impressing anyone with that car. Definitely not a babe magnet! The old slant six that Plymouth used in that car would run forever. You could really abuse them without failure. I had been told that particular engine could actually run upside down for quite a while without failure. I had never actually witnessed one of these engines running upside down, but I would not doubt it.

The car was pretty dependable for Mom; however, it did have carburetor issues. I think she'd had the car for almost a year when it developed this condition where just before you came to a stop, when you were approaching a yellow light at the intersection, the engine would stall. Once you got used to the car's personality, you would put it in neutral and start it back up as you were turning left. You had to respond quickly by throwing the transmission into neutral and turning the key to restart the engine, throwing it back into drive. You would breathe a sigh of relief when the vehicle started back up and you made it through the light with your life! My mom had this problem fixed. The repair lasted for a while, but the condition returned after about six months. It is hindsight now, but she could have kept that car for a while longer.

Her next purchase was not the best decision. She purchased a brand-new Renault Alliance in 1983, the very same year I graduated from high school. It was the first year they sold those cars in the U.S. Because it was a new model, it had no track record yet. The car was okay for a couple of years. It may have helped that she drove the car conservatively, and it did not have too many problems. The engine's cooling fan control switch was stuck on. It went unnoticed, allowing the engine's cooling fan to run constantly. Time went on and the fan motor burned out. The engine overheated, blowing a hole in the radiator and then ultimately blowing the engine's head gasket. She got the car repaired and ran it for a year longer; then I believe the transmission began to act up. I suggested that she should trade the car for a new one, which she did soon after. Renault had a recall on the Alliance for the heater core. The core could actually rupture and spray hot antifreeze on your leg! The decision was made to get rid of that car, before too much more went wrong with it. She got a new 1987 Honda Civic. This car was the last car that she owned and the best one, with no troubles.

My very first car was a white AMC Gremlin that was full of

Bondo! I purchased it for $50. It was a pretty sad-looking car. My intentions were good, but I never got it on the road. It needed a clutch, transmission, and a whole great big list of stuff! One of the things that motivated me to buy it was that a friend of mine had one with a 327 cubic inch Chevy motor in it. That car could move! Needless to say, my AMC Gremlin moved only if you pushed it! I decided not to invest any time or money into that car. I did, however, get my $50 back from the junkyard where I bought it.

I worked part-time for a cleaning company in junior high school to save up cash for a car that I could get on the road quickly. I went to Keene High School to their CVC program (Cheshire Vocational Center), for advanced automotive repair. Another student who attended CVC drove a 1972 GMC Sprint. This car resembled an El Camino, a kind of half--car/half-truck vehicle. All I knew was it had a cool orange gold color, aluminum wheels, a V-8 engine, and that I had to own that car. I bought the car for $1,700—I did not fully realize that the car's frame was badly rusted through in spots, and it had been already patched in a couple other areas as well. At this point in time, I felt pretty ill. You know that sinking feeling you get when you find out some bad news? Well, I had that feeling for sure.

If I had taken the time to arrange to have the car put up on a hoist and checked over, I could have saved myself a lot of trouble and money. My good buddy Marc's father owned a small garage in the nearby town of Gilsum N.H, and was pretty proficient at welding. He fabricated several good patches, so the car could pass state inspection. Live and learn, I guess. Me being just a kid, I did not see past the shiny paint and shiny wheels. I learned a small lesson that day. With the frame repair and lots of oil undercoating, I was able to drive the car for about three years. I sold it to a guy I worked with at the time, and explained to him fully about the vehicle's frame and the rust. He did not care about that, because the frame repair was still intact. He went on to drive the car for a year or so and then junked it. I have been asked for advice from kids in the past regarding what they should buy and what they should not buy in a vehicle. Some listen and some do not; however, life is just a learning experience. In this case my emotions took over, and I was hypnotized by the appearance of the car. If I had known then what I know now, I would not have bought that car.

I graduated from high school in 1983 and continued to work for the cleaning company, now full-time instead of part-time. My goal was to get my foot into the door of an automotive dealership, so I could eventually be a mechanic. I must have gone to every dealership in the area, only find no openings for new mechanics with little experience. At that time, mechanics were a dime a dozen, and I had little experience with automotive repairs, outside of working on my own cars. Finally, in 1985, I landed a job at a Honda dealership in the Keene, New Hampshire area, but I had to start at the bottom, washing and rust-proofing cars, cleaning the shop, and running for parts. It was the start that I needed to get my foot in the door. After a year and a half of being a wash boy I was finally allowed to do oil changes. Shortly after, I was designated as a line technician, and the rest is history.

I had been informed that one of the service advisors at the dealership had a 1977 Pontiac Le Mans for sale. He had purchased the car from a woman who bought the car brand-new from the dealership. I took a look at the car, and it was very clean inside and out. Neatly tucked away in the glove box were all the service records for the car from day one. This was a very good sign for me, so I bought the car. It was a red two-door with a half-vinyl white top. I drove that car for years without any real trouble. I later sold it to a friend of mine and he drove the car for many years after I owned it. It was definitely a boat, but it sure had a nice ride ... I kind of miss that car.

My next car was a 1980 Chevy Camaro. I kind of got upside down in the car—it was not that I could not afford the car, it was the fact that I foolishly invested way too much money into the car. I ended up having to replace the clutch right from the start, and then the engine. It had a 305 V8 engine and the camshaft went bad in it. I found a used Chevy 350 V8 engine and boy, did that car move after that! I had to get the car painted, and by the time I was done I had way too much time and money invested in it—well, way more than I planned, anyway. It was a real fun fast car and I'm very surprised that I did not get a speeding ticket in that car! I had to rid myself of the car because I purchased a house in the country on a dirt road. There was no way that the car would be practical to drive, being so low to the ground. I would definitely not be able to drive that car during mud season. Later on I finally sold it to my nephew. He promised me that he would take care of the car, and I sold it to him dirt cheap. Much to my disappointment he tried to take care of the car, but he did not have enough money or resources to do so. I am glad he had some fun with the car while he owned it, and he did not get hurt in the process.

I found a 1987 Toyota pickup with four-wheel drive to negotiate the winter months and mud season. This truck was great, except I had to do body work on it for what seemed to be every quarter of a given calendar year. I oil undercoated the heck out of it. It did not matter, as far as the bed of the truck was concerned. The frame stayed solid due to all of the oil undercoating, but the bed rusted out very quickly. I drove that truck for a lot of years with no real problems at all. I did get tired of doing all the body work to it. I did the body work one final time and traded it in for a 1997 Ford F-150.

The Ford F-150 rode nice, but it was rather unpredictable after awhile. It really was not a truck that I felt comfortable taking on long trips, especially after I had owned it for about four years—check engine lights, misfires, etc. The truck really let me down only once, and that was shortly after I bought it. This particular early production 4.6 L engine used spark plug wires instead of coil packs over each spark plug. It took me a good two hours to replace the spark plugs and wires. I did this twice in the length of time I owned the truck. My legs hurt for days afterwards from trying to crawl around the engine compartment! I had payments on this truck for only a couple of years, and then I paid it off and I drove it for many more years to come. Overall, I would have to say the Ford was a pretty good truck.

I had to finally sell the Ford F-150 and reluctantly get into another truck payment. The truck was getting up there in mileage and was becoming unpredictable, not to mention I was also getting bored with it. The truck I now own is a 2005 Toyota Tundra. I just paid the truck off, and I know that it will hold its value for many years to come. I love this truck and I am hoping to drive it for a long time to come, as well! Now I have told you a little bit about myself, and about every car I have owned since I first learned to drive. I am now forty-five and have owned seven cars since I was seventeen. At this point you realize that I keep a vehicle for as long as possible. My goal in this book is to have you do the same by educating you about how to find, purchase, and maintain your vehicle for many years of reliable safe transportation.

I have been in the auto repair business for over twenty-five years, primarily specializing in the repair and maintenance of Honda automobiles at a dealership. However, in late 2004 I decided to move on to a small independent auto repair shop. I got more exposure to all makes and models. This was okay at first. The owner was a very sharp individual and was definitely a great mechanic; however, the working conditions were substandard. Those conditions had a negative effect on my performance with diagnostics and my overall efficiency. I decided to move on to another independent automotive repair shop that has eight technicians and a more controlled atmosphere. That is where I am still currently employed to this day.

Joe Boulay achieved A.S.E master technician and Honda's platinum level status while employed as a Honda automobile technician for a total of twenty years. Then later, he gained experience on all makes and models. He hopes to help many people in the near future with this book and what he has experienced in his automotive career.

CPSIA information can be obtained at www.ICGtesting.com
Printed in the USA
BVOW071615090812

297492BV00001B/2/P